Merriam-Webster's
Pocket Guide
to
Punctuation

Merriam-Webster, Incorporated
Springfield, Massachusetts

A GENUINE MERRIAM-WEBSTER

The name *Webster* alone is no guarantee of excellence. It is used by a number of publishers and may serve mainly to mislead an unwary buyer.

Merriam-Webster™ is the name you should look for when you consider the purchase of dictionaries and other fine reference books. It carries the reputation of a company that has been publishing since 1831 and is your assurance of quality and authority.

Copyright © 1995 by Merriam-Webster, Incorporated
Philippines Copyright 1995 by Merriam-Webster, Incorporated

Library of Congress Cataloging-in-Publication Data
Pocket guide to punctuation.
    Merriam-Webster's pocket guide to punctuation.
       p.   cm.
    "Adapted from Merriam-Webster's guide to punctuation and style and various other Merriam-Webster publications"—Pref.
    Includes index.
    ISBN 0-87779-502-9
    1. English language—Punctuation—Handbooks, manuals, etc. I. Merriam-Webster, Inc. II. Title.
PE1450.P6   1995   95-4688
428.2—dc20   CIP

Printed and bound in the United States of America

456NFWP98

Contents

Preface

Merriam-Webster's Pocket Guide to Punctuation is designed to be a concise handbook on the basic conventions of written English. In addition to punctuation, it contains a brief but thorough discussion of the mechanics of English style. For each topic, the book describes the rules and practices developed by writers and editors to help them prepare copy that is clear and consistent.

This book draws on Merriam-Webster's extensive citation files of more than 14 million examples of English words used in context, and it offers readers information about both the consensus and the variety in standard American writing.

The consensus is stated categorically: for example, "A period ends a sentence or a sentence fragment that is neither interrogative nor exclamatory."

Sometimes these statements have to be qualified, as in "The abbreviations A.D. and B.C. usually appear in typeset matter as punctuated, unspaced small capitals. . . ." The term *usually* is used to indicate that a minority of writers and editors may follow a practice different from the one described. The word *sometimes* is used in describing practices that are not prevalent. The qualifiers *often* and *frequently* are used without suggesting anything about the prevalence except that the practice is not universally followed.

Merriam-Webster's Pocket Guide to Punctuation is adapted from *Merriam-Webster's Guide to Punctuation and Style* and other Merriam-Webster publications. This adaptation was carried out by Jocelyn White Franklin with assistance from Mark A. Stevens. The index was prepared by Jennifer S. Goss and Michael D. Roundy and was keyboarded by Florence A. Fowler.

Chapter 1

Punctuation

Punctuation marks are used to help clarify the structure and meaning of sentences. They separate groups of words for meaning and emphasis; they convey an idea of the variations in pitch, volume, pauses, and intonation of the spoken language; and they help avoid ambiguity. In many cases, the choice of which mark of punctuation to use will be clear and unambiguous. In other cases, the structure of a sentence may allow for several patterns of punctuation. In cases like these, varying notions of correctness have grown up, and two writers might, with equal correctness, punctuate the same sentence quite differently. In this chapter, wherever more than one pattern of punctuation may be used, each is explained. If there are reasons to prefer one over another, the reasons are presented; however, punctuation frequently requires the exercise of individual judgment and taste.

Ampersand

The ampersand (&) represents the word *and*. The ampersand is usually used in correspondence only within proper names and abbreviations.

1. The ampersand is used in the names of companies but not in the names of agencies that are part of the federal government.

   American Telephone & Telegraph Co.
   Dow Jones & Company, Inc.
   Occupational Safety and Health Administration
   Securities and Exchange Commission

In writing corporate names, writers often try to reproduce the form of the name preferred by the company (taken from an annual report or company letterhead). However, this information may not be available and, even if it is available, can lead to apparent inconsistencies if several corporate names are used. If this is the case, choose one styling, preferably the one with the ampersand, and use it in all corporate names as a substitute for *and*.

2. When ampersands are used with abbreviations in general correspondence, spaces are often left around the ampersand. Writing that makes extensive use of abbreviations, such as technical writing, more commonly omits the spacing.

> Such loans may be available at your bank or S & L.

> The R&D budget looks adequate for the next fiscal year.

3. When an ampersand is used between the last two elements in a series, the comma is omitted.

> the law firm of Shilliday, Fraser & French

Apostrophe

1. The apostrophe is used to indicate the possessive case of nouns and indefinite pronouns. For details regarding this use, see the section beginning on page 123.

2. Apostrophes are sometimes used to form plurals of letters, numerals, abbreviations, symbols, and words referred to as words. For

details regarding this use, see the section beginning on page 114.

3. Apostrophes mark omissions in contractions made of two or more words that are pronounced as one word.

> didn't
> you're
> o'clock

4. The apostrophe is used to indicate that letters have been intentionally omitted from the spelling of a word in order to reproduce a perceived pronunciation or to give a highly informal flavor to a piece of writing.

> "Get 'em while they're hot."
> The club's sign will read "Dancin' till three."

Sometimes words are so consistently spelled with an apostrophe that the spelling with the apostrophe becomes an accepted variant.

> rock 'n' roll [for *rock and roll*]
> fo'c'sle [for *forecastle*]
> bos'n [for *boatswain*]

5. Apostrophes mark the omission of digits in numerals.

> class of '95
> politics in the '90s

Writers who use the apostrophe when writing the plurals of words expressed in numerals usually avoid the use of the apostrophe illustrated in the second example above. Either they omit the apostrophe that stands for the missing figures, or they spell the word out.

> 90's   *or*   nineties   *but not*   '90's

6. Apostrophes are used to produce the inflected forms of verbs that are made of numerals or individually pronounced letters. Hyphens are sometimes used for this purpose also.

> 86'ed our proposal
> OK'ing the manuscripts

7. An apostrophe is often used to add an *-er* ending to an abbreviation, especially if some confusion might result from its absence. Hyphens are sometimes used for this purpose also. If no confusion is likely, the apostrophe is usually omitted.

> 4-H'er   IBMer
> AA'er   RVer

8. The use of apostrophes to form abbreviations (such as *ass'n* for *association* or *sec'y* for *secretary*) is avoided in most formal writing.

Brackets

1. Brackets enclose editorial comments, corrections, clarifications, or other material inserted into a text, especially into quoted matter.

This was the first time since it became law that the Twenty-first Amendment [outlining procedures for the replacement of a dead or incapacitated President or Vice President] had been invoked.

He wrote, "I am just as cheerful as when you was [sic] here."

2. Brackets enclose insertions that supply missing letters.

"If you can't persuade the P[resident], I'm sure no one can."

3. Brackets enclose insertions that take the place of words or phrases that were used in the original version of a quoted passage.

The report, entitled "A Decade of Progress," begins with a short message from President Stevens in which she notes that "the loving portraits and revealing accounts of [this report] are not intended to constitute a complete history of the decade.... Rather [they] impart the flavor of the events, developments, and achievements of this vibrant period."

4. Brackets enclose insertions that slightly alter the form of a word used in an original text.

The magazine reported that thousands of the country's children were "go[ing] to bed hungry every night."

5. Brackets are used to indicate that the capitalization or typeface of the original passage has been altered in some way.

As we point out later, "The length of a quotation usually determines whether it is run into the text or set as a block quotation. . . . [L]ength can be assessed in terms of number of words, the number of typewritten or typeset lines, or the number of sentences in the passage."

They agreed with and were encouraged by her next point: "In the past, many secretaries have been placed in positions of responsibility *without being delegated enough authority to carry out the responsibility.*" [Italics added.]

The use of brackets to indicate altered capitalization is optional in most situations. It is required only in cases where meticulous handling of original source material is crucial (particularly legal contexts).

6. **Brackets function as parentheses within parentheses.**

The company was incinerating high concentrations of pollutants (such as polychlorinated biphenyls [PCBs]) in a power boiler.

7. **Brackets are used in combination with parentheses to indicate units contained within larger units in mathematical copy. They are also used in chemical formulas.**

$x + 5[(x+y)(2x-y)]$
$Ag[Pt(NO_2)_4]$

8. **No punctuation mark (other than a period after an abbreviation) precedes bracketed material within a sentence. If punctuation is**

required, the mark is placed after the closing bracket.

> The report stated, "If we fail to find additional sources of supply [of oil and gas], our long-term growth will be limited."

9. When brackets enclose a complete sentence, the required punctuation should be placed within the brackets.

> [A paw print photographed last month in the Quabbin area has finally verified the cougar's continued existence in the Northeast.]

10. No space is left between brackets and the material they enclose or between brackets and any mark of punctuation immediately following.

Colon

The colon is a mark of introduction. It indicates that what follows it—whether a clause, a phrase, or even a single word—is tightly linked with some element that precedes it. For information on capitalizing the first word following a colon, see paragraphs 7–8 on pages 76–77.

With Phrases and Clauses

1. A colon introduces a clause or phrase that explains, illustrates, amplifies, or restates what has gone before.

> The sentence was poorly constructed: it lacked both unity and coherence.

The organization combines a tradition of excellence with a dedication to human service: educating the young, caring for the elderly, assisting in community-development programs.

Computer disks provide high-density storage capacity: hundreds of megabytes of information.

Time was running out: a decision had to be made.

2. A colon directs attention to an appositive.

The question is this: Where will we get the money?

He had only one pleasure: eating.

3. A colon is used to introduce a series. The introductory statement often includes a phrase such as *the following* or *as follows*.

The conference was attended by representatives of five nations: England, France, Belgium, Spain, and Portugal.

Anyone planning to participate should be prepared to do the following: hike five miles with a backpack, sleep on the ground without a tent, and paddle a canoe through rough water.

Opinion varies regarding whether a colon should interrupt the grammatical continuity of a clause (for example, by coming between a verb and its objects). Although many writers avoid this practice and use a full independent clause before the colon, the interrupting colon is common. It is especially likely to be used before a lengthy and complex list, where the colon serves to set the list apart from the normal flow of running text. With shorter or less complex lists, the colon is usually not used.

> Our programs to increase profitability include: continued modernization of our manufacturing facilities; consolidation of distribution terminals; discontinuation of unprofitable retail outlets; and reorganization of our personnel structure, along with across-the-board staff reductions.

> Our programs to increase profitability include plant modernization, improved distribution and retailing procedures, and staff reductions.

> Our programs to increase profitability include the following: continued modernization of our manufacturing facilities; consolidation of distribution terminals; discontinuation of unprofitable retail outlets; and reorganization of our personnel structure, along with across-the-board staff reductions.

4. A colon is used like a dash to introduce a summary statement following a series.

> Physics, biology, sociology, anthropology: she discusses them all.

With Quotations

5. A colon introduces lengthy quoted material that is set off from the rest of a text by indentation but not by quotation marks.

> He took the title for his biography of Thoreau from a passage in *Walden:*

> I long ago lost a hound, a bay horse, and a turtle-dove, and am still on their trail. ... I have met one or two who had heard the hound, and the tramp of the horse,

and even seen the dove disappear behind a cloud, and they seemed as anxious to recover them as if they had lost them themselves.

However, the title *A Hound, a Bay Horse, and a Turtle-Dove* probably puzzled some readers.

6. A colon may be used before a quotation in running text, especially when (1) the quotation is lengthy, (2) the quotation is a formal statement or is being given special emphasis, or (3) the quotation is an appositive.

Said Murdoch: "The key to the success of this project is good planning. We need to know precisely all of the steps that we will need to go through, what kind of staff we will require to accomplish each step, what the entire project will cost, and when we can expect completion."

The inscription reads: "Here lies one whose name was writ in water."

In response, he had this to say: "No one knows better than I do that changes will have to be made soon."

Other Uses

7. A colon separates elements in page references, bibliographical and biblical citations, and fixed formulas used to express time and ratios.

Journal of the American Medical Association 48:356
Stendhal, *Love* (New York: Penguin, 1975)
John 4:10
8:30 a.m.
a ratio of 3:5

8. A colon separates titles and subtitles (as of books).

> *The Tragic Dynasty: A History of the Romanovs*

9. A spaced colon is used to join terms that are being contrasted or compared.

> The budget shows an unfavorable difference in research : advertising dollars.

10. A colon punctuates the salutation in formal correspondence.

> Dear Mrs. Wright:
> Dear Laurence:
> Dear Product Manager:
> Ladies and Gentlemen:
> To whom it may concern:

11. A colon punctuates memorandum and government correspondence headings and subject lines in general business letters.

> TO: VIA:
> SUBJECT: REFERENCE:

12. A colon separates writer/dictator/typist initials in the identification lines of business letters.

> WAL:jml
> WAL:WEB:jml

13. A colon separates carbon-copy or blind carbon-copy abbreviations from the initials or names of copy recipients in business letters.

> cc:RSP   bcc:MWK
>   JES   FCM

With Other Marks of Punctuation

14. A colon is placed outside quotation marks and parentheses.

> There's only one thing wrong with "Harold's Indiscretion": it's not funny.
>
> I quote from the first edition of *Springtime in Savannah* (published in 1952):

Spacing

15. No space precedes or follows a colon when it is used between numerals.

> 9:30 a.m.
> a ratio of 2:4

16. No space precedes or follows a colon in a business-letter identification line or in a carbon-copy notation that indicates a recipient designated by initials. One space follows a colon in a carbon-copy notation that indicates a recipient designated by a full name.

> FCM:hg
> cc:FCM
> cc: Mr. Johnson

Comma

The comma is the most frequently used punctuation mark in English. Its most common uses are to separate items in a series and to set off or distinguish grammatical elements within sentences.

This section explains the most common aspects of the comma.

Between Main Clauses

1. A comma separates main clauses joined by a coordinating conjunction: *and, but, or, nor, for,* and sometimes *so* and *yet*. (For use of commas with clauses joined by correlative conjunctions, see paragraph 24 on pages 23–24.)

> She knew very little about the new system, and he volunteered nothing.
>
> We will not respond to any more questions on that topic this afternoon, nor will we respond to similar questions at any time in the future.
>
> His face showed disappointment, for he knew that he had failed.
>
> The acoustics in this hall are good, so every note is clear.
>
> We have requested this information many times before, yet we have never gotten a satisfactory reply.

2. When one or both of the clauses are short or closely related in meaning, the comma is often omitted.

> The sun was shining and the birds were singing.
>
> Six thousand years ago, the top of the volcano blew off in a series of powerful eruptions and the sides collapsed into the middle.

In punctuating sentences such as these, writers have to use their own judgment. There are no clear-cut rules to follow; however, factors such as the rhythm, parallelism, or logic of the sentence often influence how clearly or smoothly it will read with or without the comma.

3. Commas are sometimes used to separate main clauses that are not joined by conjunctions. This is especially likely if the clauses are short and obviously parallel.

> One day you are a successful corporate lawyer, the next day you are out of work.
> The city has suffered terribly in the interim. Bombs have destroyed most of the buildings, disease has ravaged the population.

Using a comma to join clauses that are neither short nor obviously parallel is usually called *comma fault* or *comma splice* and should be avoided. In general, clauses not joined by conjunctions are separated by semicolons.

4. If a sentence is composed of three or more clauses, the clauses may be separated by either commas or semicolons. Clauses that are short and free of commas can be separated by commas even if they are not joined by a conjunction. If the clauses are long or punctuated, they are separated with semicolons; the last two clauses may be separated by a comma, but usually only if they are joined by a conjunction. (For more examples of clauses separated with commas and semicolons, see paragraph 5 on page 69.)

Small fish fed among the marsh weed, ducks paddled along the surface, a muskrat ate greens along the bank.

The policy is a complex one to explain; defending it against its critics is not easy, nor is it clear the defense is always necessary.

With Compound Predicates

5. Commas are not normally used to separate the parts of a compound predicate.

The firefighter tried to enter the burning building but was turned back by the thick smoke.

However, many writers do use commas to separate the parts of a compound predicate if the predicate is especially long and complicated, if one part of the predicate is being stressed, or if the absence of a comma could cause a momentary misreading of the sentence.

The board helps to develop the financing, new product planning, and marketing strategies for new corporate divisions, and issues periodic reports on expenditures, revenues, and personnel appointments.

This is an unworkable plan, and has been from the start.

I try to explain to him what I want him to do, and get nowhere.

With Subordinate Clauses and Phrases

6. Adverbial clauses and phrases that precede a main clause are usually set off with commas.

As cars age, they depreciate.

Having made that decision, we turned our attention to other matters.

From the top of this rugged and isolated plateau, I could see the road stretching out for miles across the desert.

In addition, staff members respond to queries, take new orders, and initiate billing.

7. If a sentence begins with an adverbial clause or phrase and can be easily read without a comma following it, the comma may be omitted. In most cases where the comma is omitted, the phrase will be short—four words or less. However, the comma can be omitted even after a longer phrase if the sentence can be easily read or seems more forceful that way.

In January the company will introduce a new line of entirely redesigned products.

On the map the town appeared as a small dot in the midst of vast emptiness.

If the project cannot be done profitably perhaps it should not be done at all.

8. Adverbial clauses and phrases that introduce a main clause other than the first main clause are usually set off with commas. However, if the adverbial clause or phrase follows a conjunction, two commas are usually used: one before the conjunction and one following the clause or phrase. In some cases three commas are used: one before the conjunction and two more to enclose the clause or phrase. Some

writers use only one comma to separate the main clauses.

> His parents were against the match, and had the couple not eloped, their plans for marriage would have come to nothing.
>
> They have redecorated the entire store, but, to the delight of their customers, the store retains much of its original flavor.
>
> We haven't left Springfield yet, but when we get to Boston we'll call you.

9. A comma is not used after an introductory phrase if the phrase immediately precedes the main verb.

> In the road lay a dead rabbit.

10. A subordinate clause or phrase that follows a main clause or falls within a main clause is usually not set off by commas if it is *restrictive*—that is, if its removal from the sentence would alter the meaning of the main clause. If the meaning of the main clause would not be altered by removing the subordinate clause or phrase, the clause or phrase is considered *nonrestrictive* and usually is set off by commas.

> We will be delighted if she decides to stay. [*restrictive*]
>
> Anyone who wants his or her copy of the book autographed by the author should get in line. [*restrictive*]
>
> Her new book, which was based on a true story, was well received. [*nonrestrictive*]

That was a good meal, although I didn't particularly like the broccoli in cream sauce. [*nonrestrictive*]

11. Commas are used to set off an adverbial clause or phrase that falls between the subject and the verb.

The weather in the capital, fluctuating from very hot to downright chilly, necessitates a variety of clothing.

12. Commas set off modifying phrases that do not immediately precede the word or phrase they modify.

The negotiators, tired and discouraged, headed back to the hotel.

We could see the importance, both long-term and short-term, of her proposal.

The two children, equally happy with their lunches, set off for school.

13. Absolute phrases (phrases that stand alone and don't affect the grammar of the rest of the sentence) are set off with commas, whether they fall at the beginning, middle, or end of the sentence.

Our business being concluded, we adjourned for refreshments.

We headed southward, the wind freshening behind us, to meet the rest of the fleet in the morning.

I'm afraid of his reaction, his temper being what it is.

With Appositives

14. Commas are used to set off a word, phrase, or clause that is in apposition to (that is, equivalent to) a preceding noun and that is nonrestrictive.

> My husband, Larry, is in charge of ticket sales for the fair.

> George Washington, first president of the United States, has been the subject of countless biographies.

A nonrestrictive appositive phrase or clause sometimes precedes the noun it refers to. It is set off by commas in this position also.

> A cherished landmark in the city, the Hotel Sandburg has managed once again to escape the wrecking ball.

15. Restrictive appositives are not set off by commas.

> My daughter Andrea had the lead in the school play.

Note that if Andrea were the parent's *only* daughter, her name would be set off by commas.

With Introductory and Interrupting Elements

16. Commas set off transitional words and phrases.

> Indeed, close coordination between departments can minimize confusion during this period of expansion.

We are eager to begin construction; however, the necessary materials have not yet arrived.

The most recent report, on the other hand, makes clear why the management avoids such agreements.

When these words are not used to make a transition, no comma is necessary.

The materials had indeed arrived.

17. Commas set off parenthetical elements, such as authorial asides and supplementary information, that are closely related to the rest of the sentence.

All of us, to tell the truth, were completely amazed by his suggestion.

The headmaster, now in his sixth year at the school, was responsible for the changes in the curriculum.

When the parenthetical element is digressive or otherwise not closely related to the rest of the sentence, it is often set off by dashes or parentheses. For examples, see paragraph 3 on pages 34–35 and paragraph 1 on page 49.

18. Commas are used to set off words or phrases that introduce examples or explanations.

He expects to visit three countries, namely, France, Spain, and Germany.

I would like to develop a good, workable plan, i.e., one that would outline our goals and set a timetable for accomplishing them.

Words and phrases such as *i.e., e.g., namely, for example,* and *that is* are often preceded by a dash, open parenthesis, or semicolon, depending on the magnitude of the break in continuity created by the examples or explanations. However, regardless of the punctuation that precedes the word or phrase, a comma always follows it. For examples of dashes, parentheses, and semicolons with these words and phrases, see paragraph 6 on page 36, paragraph 2 on pages 49–50, and paragraph 6 on pages 69–70.

19. Commas are used to set off words in direct address.

> We would like to discuss your account, Mrs. Reid.
>
> The answer, my friends, lies within us.

20. Commas set off mild interjections or exclamations such as *ah* or *oh*.

> Ah, weekends—they don't come often enough.
>
> Oh, what a beautiful baby.

With Contrasting Expressions

21. A comma is used to set off contrasting expressions within a sentence.

> This project will take six months, not six weeks.

22. Style varies regarding use of the comma to set off two or more contrasting phrases used to describe a single word that follows immedi-

ately. Some writers put a comma after the
first modifier but not between the final modifier and the word modified. Other writers,
who treat the contrasting phrase as a nonrestrictive modifier, put a comma both before
and after the phrase.

> The harsh, although eminently realistic critique
> is not going to make you popular.
>> *or*
> The harsh, although eminently realistic, critique
> is not going to make you popular.
> This street takes you away from, not toward the
> capitol building.
>> *or*
> This street takes you away from, not toward, the
> capitol building.

23. Adjectives and adverbs that modify the same
word or phrase and that are joined by *but* or
some other coordinating conjunction are not
separated by a comma.

> the harsh but eminently realistic critique
> a multicolored but subdued carpet
> errors caused by working carelessly or too
> quickly

24. A comma does not usually separate elements
that are contrasted through the use of a pair
of correlative conjunctions (such as *either . . .
or, neither . . . nor,* and *not only . . . but also*).

> The cost is either $69.95 or $79.95.
> Neither my brother nor I noticed the error.

He was given the post not only because of his diplomatic connections but also because of his great tact and charm.

Correlative conjunctions are sometimes used to join main clauses. If the clauses are short, a comma is not added. If the clauses are long, a comma usually separates them.

Either you do it my way or we don't do it at all.

Not only did she have to see three salesmen and a visiting reporter during the course of the day, but she also had to prepare for the next day's meeting with the president.

25. Long parallel contrasting and comparing clauses are separated by commas; short parallel phrases are not.

The more I hear about this new computer, the greater is my desire to obtain one for my office.

"The sooner the better," I said.

With Items in a Series

26. Words, phrases, and clauses joined in a series are separated by commas. If main clauses are joined in a series, they may be separated by either semicolons or commas. (For more on the use of commas and semicolons to separate main clauses, see paragraphs 1, 3, and 4 on pages 14–16 and paragraph 5 on page 69.)

Men, women, and children crowded aboard the train.

Her job required her to pack quickly, to travel often, and to have no personal life.

He responded patiently while reporters shouted questions, flashbulbs popped, and the crowd pushed closer.

Practice varies regarding the use of the comma between the last two items in a series if those items are also joined by a conjunction. Sometimes, as in the following example, omitting the final comma (often called the *serial comma*) can result in ambiguity. Some writers feel that in most sentences the use of the conjunction makes the comma superfluous, and they favor using the comma only when a misreading could result from omitting it. Others feel that it is easier to include the final comma routinely rather than try to consider each sentence separately to decide whether a misreading is possible without the comma. Most reference books, including this one, and most other book-length works of nonfiction use the serial comma. In most other kinds of writing, however, practice is nearly evenly divided on the use or omission of this comma.

We are looking for a house with a big yard, a view of the harbor, and beach and docking privileges. [*with serial comma*]
    or
We are looking for a house with a big yard, a view of the harbor and beach and docking privileges. [*without serial comma*]

27. A comma is not used to separate items in a series that are joined with conjunctions.

I don't understand what this policy covers or doesn't cover or only partially covers.

I have talked to the president and the vice president and three other executives.

28. When the elements in a series are long or complex or consist of clauses that themselves contain commas, the elements are usually separated by semicolons, not commas. For more on this use of the semicolon, see paragraphs 7–8 on pages 70–71.

With Coordinate Modifiers

29. A comma is used to separate two or more adjectives, adverbs, or phrases that modify the same word or phrase. (For the use of commas with contrasting modifiers, see paragraphs 22 and 23 above.)

She spoke in a calm, reflective manner.
We watched the skier move smoothly, gracefully through the turns.

30. A comma is not used between two adjectives when the first modifies the combination of the second adjective plus the word or phrase it modifies.

a good used car
a small glass figurine

31. A comma is not used to separate an adverb from the adjective or adverb that it modifies.

a truly distinctive manner
running very quickly down the street

In Quotations and Questions

32. A comma separates a direct quotation from a phrase identifying its source or speaker. If the quotation is a question or an exclamation and the identifying phrase follows the quotation, the comma is replaced by a question mark or an exclamation point.

> Mary said, "I am leaving soon."
>
> "I am leaving soon," Mary said.
>
> Mary asked, "When are you going?"
>
> "When are you going?" Mary asked.
>
> "I am staying," Mary said, "even if it means missing the reception."
>
> "Don't forget the slides!" Mary shouted.

In some cases, a colon can replace a comma preceding a quotation. For more on this use of the colon, see paragraph 6 on page 11.

33. Commas are not used to set off a quotation that is an integral part of the sentence in which it appears.

> Throughout the session his only responses were "No comment" and "I don't think so."
>
> Just because he said he was "about to leave this minute" doesn't mean he actually left.

34. Practice varies regarding the use of commas to set off shorter sentences that fall within longer sentences and that do not constitute actual dialogue. These shorter sentences may be mottoes or maxims, unspoken or imaginary dialogue, or sentences referred to as sentences; and they may or may not be enclosed in quotation marks. (For more on the use of quotation marks with sentences like these, see paragraph 6 on pages 60–61.) The shorter sentence usually functions as a subject, object, or complement within the larger sentence and does not require a comma. Where quotation marks are not used, a comma may be inserted simply to mark the beginning of the shorter sentence clearly.

"The computer is down" was the response she dreaded.

He spoke with a candor that seemed to insist, This actually happened to me and in just this way.

The first rule is, When in doubt, spell it out.

When the shorter sentence functions as an appositive in the larger sentence, it is set off with a comma or commas when nonrestrictive and not when restrictive. (For more on restrictive modifiers and appositives, see paragraphs 10, 14, and 15 on pages 18–20.)

He was fond of the slogan "Every man a king, but no man wears a crown."

We had the association's motto, "We make waves," printed on our T-shirts.

35. A comma introduces a direct question, regardless of whether it is enclosed in quotation marks or if its first word is capitalized.

I wondered, what is going on here?

The question is, How do we get out of this situation?

36. The comma is omitted before quotations that are very short exclamations or representations of sounds.

> He jumped up suddenly and cried "I've got it!"

37. A comma is not used to set off indirect discourse or indirect questions introduced by a conjunction (such as *that* or *what*).

> Mary said that she was leaving.
> I wondered what was going on there.
> The clerk told me that the book I had ordered had just come in.

With Omitted Words

38. A comma indicates the omission of a word or phrase, especially in parallel constructions where the omitted word or phrase appears earlier in the sentence.

> Common stocks are preferred by some investors; bonds, by others.

39. A comma often replaces the conjunction *that*.

> The road was so steep and winding, we thought for sure we would go over the edge.
> The problem is, we don't know how to fix it.

With Addresses, Dates, and Numbers

40. A comma is used to set off the individual elements of an address except for zip codes; no punctuation appears between a state name and the zip code that follows it. If prepositions are used between the elements of the address, commas are not needed.

Mrs. Bryant may be reached at 52 Kiowa Circle, Mesa, Arizona.

Mr. Briscoe was born in Liverpool, England.

Write to the Bureau of the Census, Washington, DC 20233.

The White House is at 1600 Pennsylvania Avenue in Washington, D.C.

Some writers omit the comma that follows the name of a state (or province, country, etc.) when no other element of an address follows it, which usually occurs when a city name and state name are being used in combination to modify a noun that follows. However, retaining this comma is still the more common practice.

We visited their Enid, Oklahoma plant.

but more commonly

We visited their Enid, Oklahoma, plant.

41. Commas are used to set off the year from the day of the month. (See also paragraph 50 below.)

On October 26, 1947, the newly hired employees began work on the project.

When only the month and the year are given, the first comma is usually omitted.

In December 1903, the Wright brothers finally succeeded in keeping an airplane aloft for a few seconds.

42. A comma groups numerals into units of three in order to separate thousands, millions, and so on; however, this comma is generally not used in page numbers, street numbers, or numbers within dates. (For more on the use of the comma with numbers, see paragraphs 1–3 on pages 182–83.)

a population of 350,000
page 1419
4509 South Pleasant Street
the year 1986

With Names, Degrees, and Titles

43. A comma punctuates an inverted name.

Sagan, Deborah J.

44. A comma is often used between a surname and *Junior, Senior,* or their abbreviations. (For more on the use of *Jr.* and *Sr.*, see paragraph 44 on pages 171–72.)

Morton A. Williams, Jr.
Douglas Fairbanks, Senior

45. A comma is often used to set off the word *Incorporated* or the abbreviation *Inc.* from the rest of a corporate name; however, many companies elect to omit this comma from their names.

Leedy Manufacturing Company, Incorporated
Tektronics, Inc.
Merz-Fortunata Inc.

46. A comma separates a surname from a following academic, honorary, military, or religious degree or title.

Amelia P. Artandi, D.V.M.
Robert Menard, M.A., Ph.D.
John L. Farber, Esq.
Admiral Herman Washington, USN
Sister Mary Catherine, S.C.

In Correspondence

47. The comma follows the salutation in informal correspondence and often follows the complimentary close in both informal and formal correspondence. In formal correspondence, a colon follows the salutation. (For examples of this use of the colon, see paragraph 10 on page 12.)

Dear Rachel,
Affectionately,
Very truly yours,

Other Uses

48. The comma is used to avoid ambiguity when the juxtaposition of two words or expressions could cause confusion.

Whatever will be, will be.
To John, Marshall Inc. was a special environment.
I repaired the lamp that my brother had broken, and replaced the bulb.

49. A comma often follows a direct object or a predicate nominative or predicate adjective when they precede the subject and verb in the sentence. If the meaning of the sentence is clear without this comma, it is often omitted.

> That we would soon have to raise prices, no one disputed.
>
> A disaster it certainly was.

With Other Marks of Punctuation

50. Commas are used in conjunction with brackets, ellipsis points, parentheses, and quotation marks. Commas are not used in conjunction with colons, dashes, exclamation points, question marks, or semicolons. If one of these latter marks falls at the same point in a sentence at which a comma would fall, the comma is dropped and the other mark is retained. For more on the use of commas with other marks of punctuation, see the sections for each of those marks of punctuation.

Dash

The dash can function like a comma, a colon, or a pair of parentheses. Like commas and parentheses, dashes set off parenthetic material such as examples, supplemental facts, or appositional, explanatory, or descriptive phrases. Like colons, dashes introduce clauses that explain or expand upon some element of the material that precedes them. The dash is sometimes considered to be a less formal equivalent of the colon and parenthesis, and it does frequently take their place in advertising and other informal contexts. However, dashes may be found in all kinds of writing, including the most formal, and the choice of which mark to use is usually a matter of personal preference.

The dash exists in a number of different lengths. The most common dash is the *em dash,* which is approximately the width of a capital M in typeset material. In typed and keyboarded material, it is represented by two hyphens. Word-processing programs often have special characters for em and en dashes. The en dash and the two- and three-em dashes have more limited uses, which are explained in paragraphs 13–15 on pages 39–40.

Abrupt Change or Suspension

1. The dash marks an abrupt change or break in the structure of a sentence.

> The students seemed happy enough with the new plan, but the alumni—there was the problem.

2. A dash is used to indicate interrupted speech or a speaker's confusion or hesitation.

> "The next point I'd like to bring up—" the speaker started to say.
>
> "Yes," he went on, "yes—that is—I guess I agree."

Parenthetic and Amplifying Elements

3. Dashes are used in place of other punctuation (such as commas or parentheses) to emphasize parenthetic or amplifying material or to make such material stand out more clearly from the rest of the sentence.

> Mail your subscription—now!
>
> In 1976, they asked for—and received—substantial grants from the federal government.
>
> The privately owned consulting firm—formerly known as Aborjaily & Associates—is now offering many new services.

When dashes are used to set off parenthetic elements, they often indicate that the material is more digressive than elements set off with commas but less digressive than elements set off by parentheses. For examples, see paragraph 17 on page 21 and paragraph 1 on page 49.

4. Dashes are used to set off or to introduce defining and enumerating phrases.

> The fund sought to acquire controlling positions—a minimum of 25% of outstanding voting securities—in other companies.
>
> The essay dealt with our problems with waste—cans, bottles, discarded tires, and other trash.

5. A dash is often used in place of a colon or semicolon to link clauses, especially when the clause that follows the dash explains, summarizes, or expands upon the clause that precedes it.

> The test results were surprisingly good—none of the tested models displayed serious problems.

6. A dash or a pair of dashes often sets off parenthetic or amplifying material introduced by such phrases as *for example, namely, that is, e.g.,* and *i.e.*

> After some discussion the motion was tabled—that is, it was removed indefinitely from the board's consideration.
>
> Sports develop two valuable traits—namely, self-control and the ability to make quick decisions.
>
> Not all "prime" windows—i.e., the ones installed when a house is built—are equal in quality.

Commas, parentheses, and semicolons are often used for the same purpose. For examples, see paragraph 18 on pages 21–22, paragraph 2 on pages 49–50, and paragraph 6 on pages 69–70.

7. A dash introduces a summary statement that follows a series of words or phrases.

> Unemployment, strikes, inflation, stock prices, mortgage rates—all are part of the economy.
>
> Once into bankruptcy, the company would have to pay cash for its supplies, defer maintenance, and lay off workers—moves that could threaten its long-term profitability.

8. A dash often precedes the name of an author or source at the end of a quoted passage. This method of attribution is most often used when the quoted material—such as quotations set as epigraphs or extracts—is not part of the main text. The attribution may appear immediately after the quotation, or it may appear on the next line.

> "A comprehensive, authoritative, and beautifully written biography."—*National Review*

> Winter tames man, woman, and beast.
> —William Shakespeare

With Other Marks of Punctuation

9. If a dash appears at a point in a sentence where a comma could also appear, the dash is retained and the comma is dropped.

> If we don't succeed—and the critics say we won't—then the whole project is in jeopardy.

> Our lawyer has read the transcript—all 1,200 pages of it—and he has decided that an appeal would not be useful.

> Some of the other departments, however—particularly Accounting, Sales, and Credit Collection—have expanded their computer operations.

10. If the second of a pair of dashes would come at a point in a sentence where a period or semicolon should also appear, the period or semicolon is retained and the dash is dropped. (Writers will often avoid this construction by recasting the sentence.)

> His conduct has always been exemplary—near-perfect attendance, excellent productivity, a good attitude; nevertheless, his termination cannot be avoided.

11. Dashes are used with exclamation points and question marks. When a pair of dashes sets

off material calling for either of these marks of punctuation, the exclamation point or the question mark is placed inside the second dash.

> His hobby was getting on people's nerves—especially mine!—and he was extremely good at it.
> When the committee meets next week—are you going to be there?—I will present all of the final figures.

12. Dashes and parentheses are used in combination to indicate parenthetic material appearing within parenthetic material. Dashes within parentheses and parentheses within dashes are used with about equal frequency.

> We were looking for a narrator (or narrators—sometimes a script calls for more than one) who could handle a variety of assignments.
> On our trip south we crossed a number of major rivers—the Hudson, the Delaware, and the Patapsco (which flows through Baltimore)—without paying a single toll.

If the inner parenthetic element begins with a dash and its closing dash would fall in the same position as the closing parenthesis, the closing dash is omitted, as in the first example above. If the inner element begins with a parenthesis and its closing parenthesis would coincide with the closing dash, both are retained, as in the second example above.

En Dash

13. En dashes generally appear only in typeset material; in typed or keyboarded material the simple hyphen is usually used. The en dash is shorter than the em dash but slightly longer than the hyphen. It is most frequently used (1) as a replacement for a hyphen following a prefix that is added to an open compound, (2) as an equivalent to "(up) to and including" when used between numbers, dates, or other notations to indicate range, (3) as a replacement for the word *to* between capitalized names, and (4) to indicate linkages, such as boundaries, treaties, or oppositions.

> pre–Civil War architecture
> 1988–89
> pages 128–34
> 8:30 a.m.–4:30 p.m.
> the New York–Connecticut area
> Washington–Moscow diplomacy

Long Dashes

14. A two-em dash is used to indicate missing letters in a word and, less frequently, to indicate a missing word.

> Mr. P—— of Baltimore

15. A three-em dash indicates that a word has been left out or that an unknown word or figure is to be supplied.

The study was carried out in ———, a fast-growing Sunbelt city.

Spacing

16. Practice varies as to spacing around the dash. Some publications insert a space before and after a dash, but most do not. Either practice is acceptable.

Ellipsis Points

Ellipsis points is the name most often given to periods when they are used, usually in groups of three, to signal an omission from quoted material or to indicate a pause or trailing off of speech. Other names for periods used in this way include *ellipses, points of ellipsis,* and *suspension points*. Ellipsis points are often used in conjunction with other marks of punctuation, including periods used to mark the ends of sentences. When ellipsis points are used in this way with a terminal period, the omission is sometimes thought of as being marked by four periods. Most of the conventions described in this section are illustrated with quoted material enclosed in quotation marks. However, the conventions are equally applicable to quoted material set as extracts. In the following examples, ellipsis points indicate omission of material. In most cases, the full text from which these omissions have been made is some portion of this paragraph.

1. Ellipsis points indicate the omission of one or more words within a quoted sentence.

   > One book said, "Other names . . . include *ellipses, points of ellipsis,* and *suspension points.*"

2. Ellipsis points are usually not used to indicate the omission of words that precede the quoted portion. However, practice varies on this point, and in some formal contexts, especially those in which the quotation is introduced by a colon, ellipsis points are used.

   > The book maintained that "the omission is sometimes thought of as being marked by four periods."
   >
   > The book maintained: ". . . the omission is sometimes thought of as being marked by four periods."

3. Punctuation used in the original that falls on either side of the ellipsis points is often omitted; however, it may be retained, especially if this helps clarify the sentence.

   > According to the book, "*Ellipsis points* is the name most often given to periods when they are used . . . to signal an omission from quoted material or to indicate a pause or trailing off of speech."
   >
   > According to the book, "When ellipsis points are used in this way . . . , the omission is sometimes thought of as being marked by four periods."
   >
   > According to the book, "*Ellipsis points* is the name most often given to periods when they are used, usually in groups of three, . . . to indicate a pause or trailing off of speech."

4. If an omission includes an entire sentence within a passage, the last part of a sentence within a passage, or the first part of a sentence other than the first quoted sentence, the end punctuation preceding or following the omission is retained and is followed by three periods.

> That book says, "Other names for periods used in this way include *ellipses, points of ellipsis,* and *suspension points.* . . . When ellipsis points are used in this way with a terminal period, the omission is sometimes thought of as being marked by four periods."
>
> That book says, "*Ellipsis points* is the name given to periods when they are used, usually in groups of three, to signal an omission from quoted material. . . . Other names for periods used in this way include *ellipses, points of ellipsis,* and *suspension points.*"
>
> That book says, "Ellipsis points are often used in conjunction with other marks of punctuation, including periods used to mark ends of sentences. . . . The omission is sometimes thought of as being marked by four periods."

The capitalization of the word *The* in the third example is acceptable, even though that word did not begin a sentence in the original version. When the opening words of a quotation act as a sentence within the quotation, the first word is capitalized.

5. If the last words of a quoted sentence are omitted and if the original sentence ends with a period, that period is retained and three ellipsis points follow. However, if the original sentence ends with punctuation other than a period, the end punctuation often follows the ellipsis points, especially if it helps clarify the quotation.

> Their book said, "Ellipsis points are often used in conjunction with other marks of punctuation. . . ."
>
> He always ends his harangues with some variation on the question, "What could you have been thinking when you . . . ?"

Many writers and editors, especially when writing informally, choose to ignore the distinctions in paragraphs 4 and 5 and instead indicate all omissions by three periods, dropping all terminal periods that may precede or follow an omission.

6. Ellipsis points are used to indicate that a quoted sentence has been intentionally left unfinished. In situations such as this, the terminal period is not included.

> Read the statement beginning "*Ellipsis points* is the name most often given . . ." and then proceed to the numbered paragraphs.

7. A line of ellipsis points indicates that one or more lines of poetry have been omitted from a text. (For more on the treatment of poetry and extracts, see the section beginning on page 63.)

Whitman's attitude on the subject is revealed in these lines from "When I Heard the Learned Astronomer":

When I heard the learned astronomer,
. . . .
How soon unaccountable I became tired and sick,
Til rising and gliding out I wandered off by myself,
In the mystical moist night-air, and from time to time,
Looked up in perfect silence at the stars.

8. Ellipsis points are used to indicate faltering speech, especially if the faltering involves a long pause between words or a sentence that trails off or is intentionally left unfinished. In these kinds of sentences most writers treat the ellipsis points as terminal punctuation, thus removing the need for any other punctuation; however, some writers use other punctuation in conjunction with ellipsis points.

The speaker seemed uncertain how to answer the question. "Well, that's true . . . but even so . . . I think we can do better."

"Despite these uncertainties, we believe we can do it, but . . ."

"I mean . . ." he said, "like . . . How?"

9. Ellipsis points are sometimes used as a stylistic device to catch a reader's attention.

They think that nothing can go wrong . . . but it does.

10. Each ellipsis point is separated from other ellipsis points, adjacent punctuation (except for

quotation marks), and surrounding text by a space. If a terminal period is used with ellipsis points, it precedes them with no space before it and one space after it.

Exclamation Point

The exclamation point is used to mark a forceful comment. Heavy use can weaken its effect, so it should be used sparingly.

1. An exclamation point can punctuate a sentence, phrase, or interjection.

> This is the fourth time in a row he's been late!
> No one that I talked to—not even the accounting department!—seemed to know how the figures were calculated.
> Oh! you startled me.

2. The exclamation point replaces the question mark when an ironic or emphatic tone is more important than the actual question.

> Aren't you finished yet!
> Do you realize what you've done!
> Why me!

3. Occasionally the exclamation point is used with a question mark to indicate a very forceful question.

> How much did you say?!
> You did what!?

4. The exclamation point is enclosed within brackets, dashes, parentheses, and quotation marks when it punctuates the enclosed material rather than the sentence as a whole. It should be placed outside them when it punctuates the entire sentence.

> All of this proves—at long last!—that we were right from the start.
>
> Somehow the dog got the gate open (for the third time!) and ran into the street.
>
> He sprang to his feet and shouted "Point of order!"
>
> The correct word is "lax," not "lacks"!

5. Exclamatory phrases that occur within a sentence are set off by dashes or parentheses.

> And now our competition—get this!—wants to start sharing secrets.
>
> The board accepted most of the recommendations, but ours (alas!) was not even considered.

6. If an exclamation point falls at a place in a sentence where a comma or a terminal period could also go, the comma or period is dropped and the exclamation point is retained.

> "Absolutely not!" he snapped.
>
> She has written about 60 pages so far—and with no help!

If the exclamation point is part of a title, as of a play, book, or movie, it may be followed by a comma. If the title falls at the end of a sentence, the terminal period is usually dropped.

Marshall and Susan went to see *Oklahoma!,* and they enjoyed it very much.

His favorite management book is still *Up the Organization!*

Hyphen

1. Hyphens are used to link elements in compound words. For more on the styling of compound words, see the section beginning on page 129.

2. A hyphen marks an end-of-line division of a word when part of the word is to be carried down to the next line.

   We visited several showrooms, looked at the latest midsize cars (it wasn't a pleasant experience; prices are still high), and asked all the questions we could think of.

3. A hyphen divides letters or syllables to give the effect of stuttering, sobbing, or halting speech.

   S-s-sammy
   ah-ah-ah
   y-y-yes

4. Hyphens indicate a word spelled out letter by letter.

   p-r-o-b-a-t-i-o-n

5. A hyphen indicates that a word element is a prefix, suffix, or medial element. (For more

on using a hyphen with a prefix, see paragraph 61 on page 149.)

anti-
-ship
-o-

6. A hyphen is generally used in typed or keyboarded material as an equivalent to the phrase "(up) to and including" between numbers and dates. (In typeset material this hyphen is replaced by an en dash. For more on the use of the en dash, see paragraph 13 on page 39.)

7. Hyphens are sometimes used to produce inflected forms of verbs that are made of individually pronounced letters or to add an *-er* ending to an abbreviation; however, apostrophes are more commonly used for these purposes. (For more on these uses of the apostrophe, see paragraphs 6–7 on page 5.)

DH-ing for the White Sox
a dedicated UFO-er

Parentheses

Parentheses enclose material that is inserted into a main statement but is not intended to be an essential part of the statement. For some of the cases described below, especially those listed under the heading "Parenthetic Elements," commas and dashes are frequently used instead of parentheses. (For examples, see paragraph 17 on page 21 and paragraph 3 on pages 34–35.) In general, commas tend to be used when the inserted material is closely related, logically or grammatically, to the main clause; parentheses are more often used when the inserted material is only incidental.

Parenthetic Elements

1. Parentheses enclose phrases and clauses that provide examples, explanations, or supplementary facts or numerical data.

> Nominations for the association's principal officers (president, vice president, treasurer, and secretary) were heard and approved.
> Three old destroyers (all now out of commission) will be scrapped.
> Their first baseman was hitting well that season (.297, 84 RBIs), and their left fielder was doing well also (21 HRs, 78 RBIs).

2. Parentheses enclose phrases and clauses introduced by expressions such as *namely, that is, e.g.,* and *i.e.* Commas, dashes, and semicolons are also used to perform this function. (For examples, see paragraph 18 on pages 21–22, paragraph 6 on page 36, and paragraph 6 on pages 69–70.)

> In writing to the manufacturer, be as specific as possible (i.e., list the missing or defective parts, describe the nature of the malfunction, and

provide the name and address of the store where the unit was purchased).

3. Parentheses enclose definitions or translations in the main part of a sentence.

The company announced plans to sell off its housewares (small-appliances) business.

The hotel is located near the famous Paseo del Rio (river walk).

4. Parentheses enclose abbreviations that follow their spelled-out forms, or spelled-out forms that follow abbreviations.

She cited a ruling by the Federal Communications Commission (FCC).

They will study the disposal of PVC (polyvinyl chloride).

5. Parentheses often enclose cross-references.

Telephone ordering service is also provided (refer to the list of stores at the end of this catalog).

The diagram (Fig. 3) illustrates the action of the pump.

6. Parentheses enclose Arabic numerals that confirm a spelled-out number in a general text or in a legal document.

Delivery will be made in thirty (30) days.

The fee is Four Thousand Dollars ($4,000.00), payable to UNCO, Inc.

7. Parentheses enclose the name of a city or state that is inserted into a proper name for identification.

the Norristown (Pa.) State Hospital
the *Tulsa* (Okla.) *Tribune*

8. Some writers use parentheses to enclose personal asides.

It was largely as a result of this conference that the committee was formed (its subsequent growth in influence is another story).

9. Parentheses are used to enclose quotations that illustrate or support a statement made in the main text.

After he had had a few brushes with the police, his stepfather had him sent to jail as an incorrigible ("It will do him good").

Other Uses

10. Parentheses enclose unpunctuated numbers or letters separating and heading individual elements or items in a series within a sentence.

We must set forth (1) our new long-term goals, (2) our immediate objectives, and (3) the means at our disposal.

11. Parentheses indicate alternative terms.

Please sign and return the enclosed form(s).

12. Parentheses may be used in combination with numbers for several other purposes, such as setting off area codes in telephone numbers and indicating losses in accounting.

(413) 555-7899

Operating Profits (in millions)	
Cosmetics	26.2
Food products	47.7
Food services	54.3
Transportation	(17.7)
Sporting goods	(11.2)
Total	99.3

With Other Marks of Punctuation

13. If a parenthetic expression is an independent sentence, its first word is capitalized and a period is placed *inside* the last parenthesis. A parenthetic expression that occurs within a sentence—even if it could stand alone as a separate sentence—does not end with a period. It may, however, end with an exclamation point, a question mark, a period after an abbreviation, or a set of quotation marks. A parenthetic expression within a sentence does not require capitalization unless it is a quoted sentence.

> The discussion was held in the boardroom. (The results are still confidential.)

> Although several trade organizations worked actively against the legislation (there were at least three paid lobbyists working on Capitol Hill at any one time), the bill passed easily.

> After waiting in line for an hour (why do we do these things?), we finally left.

> The conference was held in Vancouver (that's in B.C.).

He was totally confused ("What can we do?") and refused to see anyone.

14. If a parenthetic expression within a sentence is composed of two independent clauses, capitalization is avoided and semicolons are usually used instead of periods. Independent sentences enclosed in parentheses employ normal patterns of capitalization and punctuation.

We visited several showrooms, looked at the prices (it wasn't a pleasant experience; prices in this area have not gone down), and asked all the questions we could think of.

We visited several showrooms and looked at the prices. (It wasn't a pleasant experience. Prices in this area have not gone down.) If salespeople were available, we asked all of the questions we could think of.

15. No punctuation mark (other than a period after an abbreviation) is placed before parenthetic material within a sentence; if a break is required, the punctuation is placed after the final parenthesis.

I'll get back to you tomorrow (Friday), when I have more details.

16. Parentheses sometimes appear within parentheses, although the usual practice is to replace the inner pair of parentheses with a pair of brackets. (For an example of brackets within parentheses, see paragraph 6 on page 7.)

> Checks must be drawn in U.S. dollars. (PLEASE NOTE: In accordance with U.S. Department of Treasury regulations, we cannot accept checks drawn on Canadian banks for amounts less than four U.S. dollars ($4.00). The same regulation applies to Canadian money orders.)

17. Dashes and parentheses are often used together to set off parenthetic material within a larger parenthetic element. For details and examples, see paragraph 12 on page 38.

Period

1. A period ends a sentence or a sentence fragment that is neither interrogative nor exclamatory.

> Write the letter.
> They wrote the required letters.
> Total chaos. Nothing works.

2. A period punctuates some abbreviations. (For more on the punctuation of abbreviations, see the section beginning on page 154.)

fig.	Jr.
N.W.	e.g.
Assn.	Co.
U.S.	Ph.D.
Dr.	ibid.
No.	Corp.

3. Periods are used with an individual's initials. If all of the person's initials are used instead of the name, however, the unspaced initials may be written without periods.

> F. Scott Fitzgerald
> J.F.K. *or* JFK

4. A period follows Roman and Arabic numerals and also letters when they are used without parentheses in outlines and vertical lists.

> I. Objectives
>   A. Economy
>   1. Low initial cost
>   2. Low maintenance cost
>   B. Ease of operation
> Required skills are:
> 1. Shorthand
> 2. Typing
> 3. Transcription

5. A period is placed within quotation marks even when it does not punctuate the quoted material.

> The founder was known to his employees as "the old man."
> "I said I wanted to fire him," Henry went on, "but she said, 'I don't think you have the contractual privilege to do that.' "

6. When brackets or parentheses enclose a sentence that is independent of surrounding sentences, the period is placed inside the closing parenthesis or bracket. However, when brackets or parentheses enclose a sentence that is part of a surrounding sentence, the period for the enclosed sentence is omitted.

> On Friday the government ordered a 24-hour curfew and told all journalists and photographers to leave the area. [Authorities later confiscated the film of those who did not comply.]
>
> I took a good look at her (she was standing quite close to me at the time).

7. One space follows a period that comes after an initial in a name. If a name is composed entirely of initials, no space is required; however, the usual style for such names is to omit the periods.

> Mr. H. C. Matthews
>
> L.B.J. *or* LBJ

8. No space follows an internal period within a punctuated abbreviation.

> f.o.b.   Ph.D.
>
> i.e.   A.D.
>
> M.L.S.   p.m.

Question Mark

1. The question mark terminates a direct question.

> What went wrong?
>
> "When do they arrive?" she asked.

The intent of the writer, not the word order of the sentence, determines whether or not

the sentence is a question. Polite requests that
are worded as questions, for instance, usually
take periods, because they are not really
questions. Similarly, a sentence that is intended as a question but whose word order is
that of a statement is punctuated with a question mark.

> Will you please sit down.
> He did that?

2. The question mark terminates an interrogative element that is part of a sentence. An indirect question is not followed by a question
mark.

> How did she do it? was the question on every-
> body's mind.
> She wondered, will it work?
> She wondered whether it would work.

3. The question mark punctuates each element
of a series of questions that share a single beginning and are neither numbered nor let-
tered. When the series is numbered or let-
tered, only one question mark is used, and it
is placed at the end of the series.

> Can you give us a reasonable forecast? back
> up your predictions? compare them with last
> year's earnings?
> Can you (1) give us a reasonable forecast, (2)
> back up your predictions, (3) compare them
> with last year's earnings?

4. The question mark indicates uncertainty about a fact.

> Geoffrey Chaucer, English poet (1340?–1400)

5. The question mark is placed inside a closing bracket, dash, parenthesis, or pair of quotation marks when it punctuates only the material enclosed by that mark and not the sentence as a whole. It is placed outside that mark when it punctuates the entire sentence.

> What did Andrew mean when he called the project "a fiasco from the start"?
>
> I took a vacation in 1989 (was it really that long ago?), but I haven't had time for one since.
>
> He asked, "Do you realize the extent of the problem [the housing shortage]?"

Quotation Marks, Double

The following paragraphs describe the use of quotation marks to enclose quoted matter in regular text, to enclose translations of words, or to enclose single letters within sentences. For the use of quotation marks or italics to enclose titles of poems, paintings, or other works, see paragraphs 77 and 82 on pages 104–5 and 106.

Basic Uses

1. Quotation marks enclose direct quotations but not indirect quotations.

> She said, "I am leaving for Frankfurt Monday."

"I am leaving Monday," she said, "and I'm not coming back until the 1st."

"I am leaving," she said. "This meeting could go on forever."

She said that she was leaving.

2. Quotation marks enclose fragments of quoted matter when they are reproduced exactly as originally stated.

> The agreement makes it clear that he "will be paid only upon receipt of an acceptable manuscript."
>
> As late as 1754, documents refer to him as "yeoman" and "husbandman."

3. Quotation marks enclose words or phrases borrowed from others, words used in a special way, or words of marked informality when they are introduced into formal writing.

> That kind of corporation is referred to as "closed" or "privately held."
>
> Be sure to send a copy of your résumé, or as some folks would say, your "biodata summary."
>
> They were afraid the patient had "stroked out"—had had a cerebrovascular accident.

4. Quotation marks are sometimes used to enclose words referred to as words. Italic type or underlining is also frequently used for this purpose. (For more on this use of italics, see paragraph 4 on page 111.)

He went through the manuscript and changed every "he" to "she."

5. Quotation marks enclose short exclamations or representations of sounds. Representations of sounds are also frequently set in italic type or underlined. (For more on this use of italics, see paragraph 6 on page 112.)

"Ssshh!" she hissed.
They never say anything crude like "shaddap."

6. Quotation marks enclose short sentences that fall within longer sentences, especially when the shorter sentence is meant to suggest spoken dialogue. Kinds of sentences that may be treated in this way include mottoes and maxims, unspoken or imaginary dialogue, and sentences referred to as sentences.

Throughout the camp, the spirit was "We can do."
She never could get used to their "That's the way it goes" attitude.
In effect, the voters were saying "You blew it, and you don't get another chance."
Their reaction could only be described as "Kill the messenger."

Some writers omit the quotation marks in sentences whose structure is clear without them. However, in general, quotation marks set the shorter sentence off more distinctly and convey more of the feel of spoken dialogue. (For more on the use of commas in sentences like these, see paragraphs 32–34 on pages 27–28.)

> The first rule is, When in doubt, spell it out.
>
> They weren't happy with the impression she left: "Don't expect favors, because I don't have to give them."

7. Quotation marks are not used to enclose paraphrases.

> Build a better mousetrap, Emerson says, and the world will beat a path to your door.

8. Direct questions are usually not enclosed in quotation marks unless they represent quoted dialogue.

> As we listened to him, we couldn't help wondering, Where's the plan?
>
> The question is, What went wrong?
>
> She asked, "What went wrong?"

As in the sentences presented in paragraph 6 above, style varies regarding the use of quotation marks with direct questions, and writers will often include the quotation marks.

> As we listened to him, we couldn't help wondering, "Where's the plan?"

9. Quotation marks are used to enclose translations of foreign or borrowed terms.

> The term *sesquipedalian* comes from the Latin word *sesquipedalis*, meaning "a foot and a half long."
>
> While in Texas, he encountered the armadillo ("little armored one").

10. Quotation marks are sometimes used to enclose single letters within a sentence.

> The letter "m" is wider than the letter "i."
> Put an "x" in the right spot.
> The metal rod was shaped into a "V."

However, practice varies on this point. Letters referred to as letters are commonly set in italic type or underlined. (For more on this use of italics, see paragraphs 4–5 on pages 111–12.) Letters often appear undifferentiated from the surrounding text where no confusion would result.

> How many *e*'s are in her name?
> a V-shaped blade
> He was happy to get a B in the course.

With Other Marks of Punctuation

11. When quotation marks follow a word in a sentence that is also followed by a period or comma, the period or comma is placed within the quotation marks.

> He said, "I am leaving."
> The packages are labeled "Handle with Care."
> The cameras were described as "waterproof," but "moisture-resistant" would have been a better description.

12. When quotation marks follow a word in a sentence that is also followed by a colon or semicolon, the colon or semicolon is placed outside the quotation marks.

There was only one thing to do when he said, "I may not run": promise him a larger campaign contribution.

She spoke of her "little cottage in the country"; she might better have called it a mansion.

13. The dash, question mark, and exclamation point are placed inside quotation marks when they punctuate the quoted matter only. They are placed outside the quotation marks when they punctuate the whole sentence.

He asked, "When did they leave?"

What is the meaning of "the open door"?

Save us from his "mercy"!

"I can't see how—" he started to say.

He thought he knew where he was going—he remembered her saying, "Take two lefts, then stay to the right"—but the streets didn't look familiar.

With Extracts

14. Quotation marks are not used with longer passages of prose or poetry that are indented as separate paragraphs, called *extracts* or *block quotations*. Extracts, as opposed to run-in quotations, are usually longer than a sentence or run to at least four lines, but individual situations of clarity and emphasis may alter these limits. Extracts are set off from the normal text by (1) indenting the passage and (2) setting it in smaller type. Extracts are usually preceded by a sentence ending with a colon, and they begin with a capitalized first word.

For information on using ellipsis points to show omissions within extracts, see the section beginning on page 40.

The chapter begins with a general description of interoffice memorandums:

> The interoffice memorandum or memo is a means of informal communication within a firm or organization. Its special arrangement replaces the salutation, complimentary close, and written signature of the letter with identifying headings.

If the extract continues the flow of an incomplete sentence, no punctuation is required and a lowercase letter can introduce the extract.

They describe the interoffice memorandum as

> a means of informal communication within a firm or organization. Its special arrangement replaces the salutation, complimentary close, and written signature of the letter with identifying headings.

If the sentence preceding the extract does not refer directly to it, the sentence ends with a period.

> As of the end of April she believed that the product had been introduced well and that it stood a good chance of success.

> Unit sales are strong, revenues are better than forecast, shipments are being made on schedule, and inventory levels are stable.

When poetic lines are set as extracts, the lines are divided exactly as in the original; a spaced slash separates lines of run-in poetry.

The experience was one that reminded them of the wisdom of Pope's observation:

> A little learning is a dang'rous thing;
> Drink deep, or taste not the Pierian spring:
> There shallow draughts intoxicate the brain,
> And drinking largely sobers us again.

When Gerard Manley Hopkins wrote that "Nothing is so beautiful as spring— / When weeds, in wheels, shoot long and lovely and lush," he probably had my yard in mind.

15. When an extract itself includes quoted material, double quotation marks enclose the material.

> The authors of the book recommend the following procedures for handling reports:
>
> > The presiding officer will call for the appropriate report from an officer, a board member, a standing committee, or a special committee by saying, "Will the chairperson of the Ways and Means Committee please present the committee's report?" After the report is presented, a motion is heard to accept the report.

16. Quotation marks are not used with an epigraph set off like an extract.

> The whole of science is nothing more than a refinement of everyday thinking.
> —Albert Einstein

Quotation Marks, Single

1. Single quotation marks enclose a quotation within a quotation. When both single and double quotation marks occur at the end of a sentence, the period typically falls within *both* sets of marks.

> The witness said, "I distinctly heard him say, 'Don't be late,' and then I heard the door close."
> The witness said, "I distinctly heard him say, 'Don't be late.' "

2. Single quotation marks are occasionally used in place of double quotation marks. This is far more common in British usage.

> The witness said, 'I distinctly heard him say, "Don't be late," and then I heard the door close.'

3. On rare occasions, writers face the question of how to punctuate a quotation within a quotation within a quotation. Standard practice would be to enclose the innermost quotation in double marks; however, this can be confusing, and rewriting the sentence can often remove the need for it.

> The witness said, "I distinctly heard him say, 'Don't you say "Shut up" to me.' "
> The witness said that she distinctly heard him say, "Don't you say 'Shut up' to me."

Semicolon

The semicolon is used in ways similar to those in which periods and commas are used. Like a period, the semicolon marks the end of a complete clause, but it also signals that the clause that follows it is closely related to the one that precedes it. The semicolon is also used to distinguish major divisions from the minor pauses that are represented by commas.

Between Clauses

1. A semicolon separates independent clauses that are joined together in one sentence without a coordinating conjunction.

> The river rose and overflowed its banks; roads became flooded and impassable; freshly plowed fields disappeared from sight.
>
> Cream the shortening and sugar; add the eggs and beat well.

2. Ordinarily a comma separates main clauses joined with a coordinating conjunction. However, if the sentence might be confusing with a comma in this position, a semicolon is used in its place. Potentially confusing sentences include those with other commas in them or with particularly long clauses.

> We fear that this situation may, in fact, occur; but we don't know when.
>
> In a society that seeks to promote social goals, government will play a powerful role; and taxation, once simply a means of raising money, becomes, in addition, a way of furthering those goals.

3. A semicolon joins two statements when the grammatical construction of the second clause is elliptical and depends on that of the first.

> The veal dishes were very good; the desserts, too.
>
> In many cases the conference sessions, which were designed to allow for full discussions of topics, were much too long and tedious; the breaks between them, much too short.

4. A semicolon joins two clauses when the second begins with a conjunctive adverb, such as *accordingly, however, indeed,* and *thus.* Phrases such as *in that case, as a result,* and *on the other hand* can also act as conjunctive adverbs. (For more on conjunctive adverbs, see the section beginning on page 226.)

> Most people are covered by insurance of one kind or another; indeed, many people don't even see their medical bills.
>
> It won't be easy to sort out the facts; however, a decision must be made.
>
> The case could take years to work its way through the court system; as a result, many plantiffs will accept out-of-court settlements.

Practice varies regarding the treatment of clauses introduced by *so* and *yet.* Although many writers continue to treat *so* and *yet* as adverbs, it has become standard to treat these words as coordinating conjunctions that join clauses. In this treatment, a comma precedes *so* and *yet* and no punctuation follows them. (For examples, see paragraph 1 on page 14.)

5. When three or more clauses are separated by semicolons, and a coordinating conjunction precedes the final clause, the final semicolon is often replaced with a comma. (For the use of commas to separate three or more clauses without conjunctions, see paragraph 4 on pages 15–16.)

> They don't understand; they grow bored; and they stop learning.
>
> The report recounted events leading up to this incident; it included observations of eyewitnesses, but it drew no conclusions.

The choice of whether or not to use a conjunction, and whether to use a semicolon or a comma with the conjunction, are matters of personal preference. In general, the semicolon makes the transition to the final clause more abrupt, which often serves to place more emphasis on that clause. The comma and conjunction ease the transition and make the sentence seem less choppy.

With Introductory Expressions

6. A semicolon is sometimes used before expressions (such as *for example, for instance, that is, namely, e.g.,* or *i.e.*) that introduce expansions or series. Commas, dashes, and parentheses are also used in sentences like these. (For examples, see paragraph 18 on pages 21–22, paragraph 6 on page 36, and paragraph 2 on pages 49–50.)

On one point only did everyone agree; namely, too much money had been spent already.

We were fairly successful on that project; that is, we made our deadlines and met our budget.

Most had traveled great distances to participate; for example, three had come from Australia, one from Japan, and two from China.

In a Series

7. A semicolon is used in place of a comma to separate phrases in a series when the phrases themselves contain commas. A comma may replace the semicolon before the last item in a series if the last item is introduced with a conjunction.

The visitor to Barndale can choose from three sources of overnight accommodation: The Rose and Anchor, which houses Barndale's oldest pub; The Crawford, an American-style luxury hotel; and Ellen's Bed and Breakfast on Peabody Lane.

We studied mathematics in the morning; English, French, and Spanish right after lunch, and science in the late afternoon.

8. When the individual items in an enumeration or series are long or are sentences themselves, they are usually separated by semicolons.

Among the committee's recommendations were the following: more hospital beds in urban areas where there are waiting lines for elective surgery; smaller staff size in half-empty rural hospitals; review procedures for all major purchases.

9. A semicolon separates items in a list in cases where a comma alone would not clearly separate the items or references.

The votes against were: Precinct 1, 338; Precinct 2, 627; Precinct 3, 514.

(Friedlander 1957; Ballas 1962)

With Other Marks of Punctuation

10. A semicolon is placed outside quotation marks and parentheses.

They referred to each other as "Mother" and "Father"; they were the archetypal happily married elderly couple.

She accepted the situation with every appearance of equanimity (but with some inward qualms); however, all of that changed the next day.

Slash

The slash is known by many names, including *virgule, diagonal, solidus, oblique,* and *slant.* Most commonly, the slash is used to represent a word that is not written out or to separate or set off certain adjacent elements of text.

In Place of Missing Words

1. A slash represents the words *per* or *to* when used with units of measure or when used to indicate the terms of a ratio.

40,000 tons/year
9 ft./sec.
price/earnings ratio
a 50/50 split

2. A slash separates alternatives. In this context, the slash usually represents the words *or* or *and/or.*

alumni/ae
his/her
oral/written tests

3. A slash replaces the word *and* in some compound terms.

molybdenum/vanadium steel
in the May/June issue
1993/94
an innovative classroom/laboratory

4. A slash is used, although less commonly, to replace a number of prepositions, such as *at, versus, with,* and *for.*

U.C./Berkeley	parent/child issues
table/mirror	Vice President/Editorial

With Abbreviations

5. A slash punctuates some abbreviations.

c/o	V/STOL
A/R	d/b/a
I/O	P/E

In some cases the slash may stand for a word that is not represented in the abbreviation (e.g., *in* in *W/O*, the abbreviation for *water in oil*).

To Separate Elements

6. The slash may be used in a number of different ways to separate groups of numbers, such as elements in a date and numerators and denominators in fractions.

7. The slash serves as a divider between lines of poetry that are run in with the text around them. This method of quoting poetry is usually limited to passages of no more than three or four lines. Longer passages are usually set off from the text as extract quotations.

> When Samuel Taylor Coleridge wrote in "Christabel" that "'Tis a month before the month of May,/And the Spring comes slowly up this way," he could have been describing New England.

Spacing

8. In general, no space is used between the slash and the words, letters, or figures separated by it; however, some writers do prefer to place spaces around a slash used to separate lines of poetry.

Chapter 2

Capitals, Italics, and Quotation Marks

Words and phrases are capitalized, italicized or underlined (underlining in typed or handwritten material is equivalent to italics in keyboarded or typeset material), or enclosed in quotation marks in order to indicate that they have a special significance in particular contexts. This chapter is divided into four sections that describe these contexts. The first section explains the use of capitalized words to begin sentences and phrases. The second explains the use of capitals, italics, and quotation marks to indicate that a word or phrase is a proper noun, pronoun, or adjective. The third and fourth sections explain other uses of capital letters and italics. For other uses of quotation marks, see the section beginning on page 58.

Beginnings

1. The first word of a sentence or sentence fragment is capitalized.

> The meeting was postponed.
> No! I can't do it.
> Total chaos. Nothing works.

2. The first word of a sentence contained within parentheses is capitalized. However, a parenthetical sentence occurring inside another sentence is not capitalized unless it is a complete quoted sentence.

> The discussion was held in the boardroom. (The results are still confidential.)
> Although we liked the restaurant (the seafood was especially good), we could not afford to go there often.
> After waiting in line for an hour (why do we do these things?), we finally left.
> He was totally demoralized ("There is just nothing we can do") and was contemplating resignation.

3. The first word of a direct quotation is capitalized. However, if the quotation is interrupted in midsentence, the second part does not begin with a capital.

> The President said, "We have rejected this report entirely."
> "We have rejected this report entirely," the President said, "and we will not comment on it further."

4. When a quotation, whether a sentence fragment or a complete sentence, is syntactically dependent on the sentence in which it occurs, the quotation does not begin with a capital.

> The President made it clear that "there is no room for compromise."

5. The first word of a sentence within a sentence is usually capitalized. Examples of sentences within sentences include mottoes and rules, unspoken or imaginary dialogue, sentences referred to as sentences, and direct questions. (For an explanation of the use of commas and quotation marks with sentences such as these, see paragraphs 34–35 on pages 27–28 and paragraphs 6 and 8 on pages 60–61.)

> You know the saying "Honesty is the best policy."
> The first rule is, When in doubt, spell it out.
> The clear message coming back from the audience was "We don't care."
> My question is, When can we go?

6. The first word of a line of poetry is usually capitalized.

> The best lack all conviction, while the worst
> Are full of passionate intensity.
> —W. B. Yeats

7. The first word following a colon may be either lowercased or capitalized if it introduces a complete sentence. While the former is the usual style, the latter is also common, especially when the sentence introduced by the colon is lengthy and distinctly separate from the preceding clause.

The advantage of this particular system is clear: it's inexpensive.

The situation is critical: This company cannot hope to recoup the fourth-quarter losses that were sustained in five operating divisions.

8. If a colon introduces a series of sentences, the first word of each sentence is capitalized.

Consider the following steps that we have taken: A subcommittee has been formed to evaluate our past performance and to report its findings to the full organization. New sources of revenue are being explored, and relevant organizations are being contacted. And several candidates have been interviewed for the new post of executive director.

9. The first words of run-in enumerations that form complete sentences are capitalized, as are the first words of vertical lists and enumerations. Numbered phrases *within* a sentence, however, are lowercased.

Do the following at the end of the day: 1. Turn off your computer. 2. Clear your desktop of papers. 3. Cover office machines. 4. Straighten the contents of cabinets and bookcases.

This is the agenda:
Call to order
Roll call
Minutes of the previous meeting
Treasurer's report

> On the agenda will be (1) call to order, (2) roll call, (3) minutes of the previous meeting, (4) treasurer's report . . .

10. In minutes and legislation, the introductory words *Whereas* and *Resolved* are capitalized (and *Resolved* is also italicized). The word *That* or an alternative word or expression which immediately follows *Whereas* or *Resolved* has its first letter capitalized.

> Whereas, Substantial benefits . . .
> *Resolved,* That . . .

11. The first word in an outline heading is capitalized.

> I. Editorial tasks
> II. Production responsibilities
>   A. Cost estimates
>   B. Bids

12. The first word of the salutation of a letter and the first word of a complimentary close are capitalized.

> Dear Mary,   Sincerely yours,
> Ladies and Gentlemen: Very truly yours,

13. The first word and each subsequent major word following a SUBJECT or TO heading (as in a memorandum) are capitalized.

> SUBJECT: Pension Plans
> TO: All Department Heads and Editors

Proper Nouns, Pronouns, and Adjectives

The following paragraphs describe the ways in which a broad range of proper nouns, pronouns, and adjectives are styled—with capitals, italics, quotation marks, or some combination of these devices. In almost all cases, proper nouns, pronouns, and adjectives are capitalized. In many cases, proper nouns are italicized (or underlined in typed or handwritten material) or enclosed in quotation marks in addition to being capitalized. No clear distinctions can be drawn between the kinds of words that are capitalized and italicized, capitalized and enclosed in quotation marks, or simply capitalized.

Abbreviations

1. Abbreviated forms of proper nouns and adjectives are capitalized, just as the spelled-out forms would be. (For more on the capitalization of abbreviations, see the section beginning on page 156.)

   Dec. [for *December*]
   Col. [for *Colonel*]
   Wed. [for *Wednesday*]
   Brit. [for *British*]

Abstractions and Personifications

2. Abstract terms, such as names of concepts or qualities, are usually not capitalized unless

the concept or quality is being presented as if it were a person. If the term is simply being used in conjunction with other words that allude to human characteristics or qualities, it is usually not capitalized. (For more on the capitalization of abstract terms, see paragraph 2 on page 109.)

> a time when Peace walked among us
> as Autumn paints each leaf in fiery colors
> an economy gripped by inflation
> hoping that fate would lend a hand

3. Fictitious names used as personifications are capitalized.

> Uncle Sam
> Ma Bell
> Jack Frost

Academic Degrees

4. The names of academic degrees are capitalized when they follow a person's name. The names of specific academic degrees not following a person's name may be capitalized or not capitalized, according to individual preference. General terms referring to degrees, such as *doctorate, master's degree,* or *bachelor's,* are not capitalized. Abbreviations for academic degrees are always capitalized.

> E. Terence Ford, Doctor of Divinity
> earned her Doctor of Laws degree
> *or*   earned her doctor of laws degree
> working for a bachelor's degree

Susan Wycliff, M.S.W.
received her Ph.D.

Animals and Plants

5. The common names of animals and plants
are not capitalized unless they contain a
proper noun as a separate element, in which
case the proper noun is capitalized and elements preceding (but not following) the
proper noun are usually but not always capitalized. If the common name contains a word
that was once a proper noun but is no longer
thought of as such, the word is usually not
capitalized. When in doubt, consult a dictionary. (For the capitalization of scientific
names, see paragraphs 66–72 on pages 101–
103.)

cocker spaniel	Great Dane
lily of the valley	black-eyed Susan
Bengal tiger	ponderosa pine
Rhode Island red	holstein

In references to specific breeds, as distinguished from the animals that belong to the
breed, all elements of the name are capitalized.

Gordon Setter
Rhode Island Red
Holstein

Awards, Honors, and Prizes

6. Names of awards, honors, and prizes are capitalized. Descriptive words and phrases that

are not actually part of the award's name are
lowercased. (For capitalizing the names of
military decorations, see paragraph 44 on
pages 93–94.)

Academy Award	Nobel Prize winner
Emmy	Nobel Prize in
Rhodes Scholarship	medicine
Rhodes scholar	Nobel Peace Prize

Derivatives of Proper Names

7. Derivatives of proper names are capitalized
when they are used in their primary sense.
However, if the derived term has taken on a
specialized meaning, it is usually not capitalized.

Roman architecture	manila envelope
Victorian customs	pasteurized milk
an Americanism	french fries

Geographical References

8. Terms that identify divisions of the earth's
surface and distinct areas, regions, places,
or districts are capitalized, as are derivative
nouns and adjectives.

the Great Plains	the Southwest
the Mariana Trench	Chicago, Illinois
the Riviera	the Middle Eastern
	situation

9. Popular names of localities are capitalized.

the Big Apple	the Twin Cities
the Village	Hell's Kitchen
the Loop	the Valley

10. Compass points are capitalized when they refer to a geographical region or when they are part of a street name. They are lowercased when they refer to a simple direction.

back East	east of the Mississippi
out West	traveling north on I-91
West Oak Street	

11. Nouns and adjectives that are derived from compass points and that designate or refer to a specific geographical region are usually capitalized.

a Southern accent
Northerners
a Western crop
part of the Eastern establishment

12. Words designating global, national, regional, or local political divisions are capitalized when they are essential elements of specific names. However, they are usually lowercased when they precede a proper name or when they are not part of a specific name.

the British Empire	New York City
the fall of the empire	the city of New York
Washington State	Ward 1
the state of Washington	fires in three wards

In legal documents, these words are often capitalized regardless of position.

the State of Washington
the City of New York

13. Common geographical terms (such as *lake, mountain, river, valley*) are capitalized if they are part of a specific proper name.

Crater Lake	Hudson Bay
Lake Como	Ohio Valley
Rocky Mountains	Great Barrier Reef
the Columbia River	Strait of Gibraltar

14. Common geographical terms preceding names are usually capitalized.

Lakes Mead and Powell
Mounts Whitney and Shasta

When *the* precedes the common term, the term is lowercased.

the river Thames

15. Common geographical terms that are not used as part of a proper name are not capitalized. These include plural terms that follow two or more proper names and terms that are used descriptively or alone.

the Himalaya and Andes mountains
the Missouri and Platte rivers
the Atlantic coast of Labrador
the Caribbean islands
the river valley

16. The names of streets, monuments, parks, landmarks, well-known buildings, and other public places are capitalized. However, common terms that are part of these names (such as *avenue, park,* or *bridge*) are lowercased when they occur after multiple names or are used alone (but see paragraph 17 below).

Fifth Avenue	Rock Creek Park
Fifth and Park avenues	walking to the park
	Golden Gate Bridge
the Pyramids	on the bridge
the Capitol	

17. Well-known informal or shortened forms of place-names are capitalized.

the Avenue [for *Fifth Avenue*]
the Street [for *Wall Street*]
the Exchange [for the *New York Stock Exchange*]

Governmental and Political Bodies

18. Full names of legislative, deliberative, executive, and administrative bodies are capitalized, as are easily recognizable short forms of these names. However, nonspecific noun and adjective references to them are usually lowercased.

United States Congress
Congress
the House
congressional hearings
the Federal Bureau of Investigation
a federal agency

When words such as *department, committee,* or *agency* are used in place of the full name of a specific body, they are most often capitalized when the department or agency is referring to itself in print; in most other cases, these words are lowercased.

> The Connecticut Department of Transportation is pleased to offer this new booklet on traffic safety. The Department hopes that it will be of use to all drivers.
>
> We received a new booklet from the Connecticut Department of Transportation. This is the second pamphlet the department has issued this month.

19. The full and short names of the U.S. Supreme Court are capitalized.

> The Supreme Court of the United States
> the United States Supreme Court
> the Supreme Court
> the Court

20. Official and full names of higher courts and names of international courts are capitalized. Short forms of official higher-court names are often capitalized in legal documents but lowercased in general writing.

> The International Court of Arbitration
> the United States Court of Appeals for the Second Circuit
> the Virginia Supreme Court
> the Court of Queen's Bench
> a ruling by the court of appeals
> the state supreme court

21. Names of city and county courts are usually lowercased.

the Lawton municipal court
the Owensville night court
small-claims court
the county court
juvenile court

22. The designation *court,* when it applies to a specific judge or presiding officer, is capitalized.

It is the opinion of this Court that . . .
The Court found that . . .

23. The terms *federal* and *national* are capitalized only when they are essential elements of a name or title.

Federal Trade Commission
federal court
National Security Council
national security

24. The word *administration* is capitalized by some writers when it refers to the administration of a specific U.S. president, but is more commonly lowercased. If the word does not refer to a specific presidency, it is not capitalized except when it is a part of the official name of a government agency.

the Truman administration
or the Truman Administration
the administration *or* the Administration
the Farmers Home Loan Administration
The running of the White House varies considerably from one administration to another.

25. Names of political organizations and their adherents are capitalized, but the word *party* may or may not be capitalized, depending on the writer's preference.

>   the Democratic National Committee
>   the Republican platform
>   Tories
>   Nazis
>   the Democratic party   *or*   the Democratic Party

26. Names of political groups other than parties are usually lowercased, as are their derivative forms.

>   the right wing
>   the liberals
>   *but usually*
>   the Left
>   the Right

27. Terms describing political and economic philosophies and their derivative forms are usually capitalized only if they are derived from proper names.

>   authoritarianism   civil libertarian
>   democracy   Marxist
>   nationalism   fascism   *or*   Fascism

Historical Periods and Events

28. The names of conferences, councils, expositions, and specific sporting, historical, and cultural events are capitalized.

>   the Yalta Conference
>   the Minnesota State Fair

> the World Series
> the Series
> the San Francisco Earthquake
> the Boston Tea Party
> the Philadelphia Folk Festival

29. The names of some historical and cultural periods and movements are capitalized. When in doubt, consult a dictionary or encyclopedia.

the Augustan Age	the Great Depression
Prohibition	fin de siècle
the Renaissance	the space age
the Enlightenment	the cold war
the Stone Age	*or* the Cold War

30. Numerical designations of historical time periods are capitalized only when they are part of a proper name; otherwise they are lowercased.

> the Roaring Twenties
> the Third Reich
> the seventeenth century
> the eighties

31. Full names of treaties, laws, and acts are capitalized.

> Treaty of Versailles
> The Clean Air Act of 1990

32. The full names of wars are capitalized. However, words such as *war, revolution, battle,* and *campaign* are capitalized only when they are part of a proper name. Descriptive terms such as *assault, siege,* and *engagement* are usually lowercased even when used in conjunction with the name of the place where the action occurred.

the French and Indian War
the Battle of the Bulge
the Peninsular Campaign
the American and French revolutions
the second battle of Manassas
the siege of Yorktown
the winter campaign
through most of the war

Hyphenated Compounds

33. Elements of hyphenated compounds are generally capitalized only if they are proper nouns or adjectives.

Arab-Israeli negotiations
East-West trade agreements
French-speaking peoples
Thirty-second Street
an eighteenth-century poet

34. Word elements (such as prefixes and combining forms) may or may not be capitalized when joined to a proper noun or adjective. Common prefixes (such as *pre-* or *anti-*) are usually not capitalized in such cases. Geographical and ethnic combining forms (such as *Anglo-* or *Sino-*) are capitalized; *pan-* is usually capitalized when attached to a proper noun or adjective.

the anti-Yeltsin faction
African-Americans
Greco-Roman architecture
Sino-Japanese relations
Pan-Slavic nationalism

Legal Material

35. The names of both plaintiff and defendant in legal case titles are italicized (or underlined in typewritten material). The *v.* (for *versus*) may be roman or italic. Cases that do not involve two opposing parties have titles such as *In re Watson* or *In the matter of John Watson,* which are also italicized. When the person involved rather than the case itself is being discussed, the reference is not italicized.

> *Jones* v. *Massachusetts*
> *In re Jones*
> *Smith et al. v. Jones*
> She covered the Jones trial for the newspaper.

In running text, a case name involving two opposing parties may be shortened.

> The judge based his ruling on a precedent set in the *Jones* decision.

Medical Terms

36. Proper names that are elements in terms designating diseases, symptoms, syndromes, and tests are capitalized. Common nouns are lowercased.

> Parkinson's disease
> Down's Syndrome

German measles
Rorschach test
mumps
herpes simplex

37. Scientific names of disease-causing organisms follow the rules discussed in paragraph 66 on page 101. The names of diseases or conditions derived from scientific names of organisms are lowercased and not italicized.

a neurotoxin produced by *Clostridium botulinum*
nearly died of botulism

38. Generic names of drugs are lowercased; trade names should be capitalized.

a prescription for chlorpromazine
had been taking Thorazine

Military Terms

39. The full titles of branches of the armed forces are capitalized, as are easily recognized short forms.

U.S. Marine Corps   the Marines
the Marine Corps   the Corps

40. The terms *air force, army, coast guard, marine(s),* and *navy* are lowercased unless they form part of an official name or refer back to a specific branch of the armed forces previously named. They are also lowercased when they are used collectively or in the plural.

the combined air forces of the NATO nations
the navies of the world
the American army

41. The adjectives *naval* and *marine* are lower-cased unless they are part of a proper name.

naval battle
marine barracks
Naval Reserves

42. The full titles of units and organizations of the armed forces are capitalized. Elements of full titles are often lowercased when they stand alone.

U.S. Army Corps of Engineers
the Reserves
a reserve commission
First Battalion
the battalion

43. Military ranks are capitalized when they precede the names of their holders, and when they take the place of a person's name (as in direct address). Otherwise they are lowercased.

General Colin Powell
I can't get this rifle any cleaner, Sergeant.
The major arrived precisely on time.

44. The specific names of decorations, citations, and medals are capitalized.

Medal of Honor
Navy Cross

Purple Heart
Distinguished Service Medal

Numerical Designations

45. A noun introducing a reference number is usually capitalized.

Order 704   Form 2E
Flight 409   Policy 118-4-Y

46. Nouns used with numbers or letters to designate major reference headings (as in a literary work) are capitalized. However, nouns designating minor reference headings are typically lowercased.

Book II   page 101
Volume V   line 8
Division 4   paragraph 6.1
Chapter 2   item 16
Table 3   question 21

Organizations

47. Names of firms, corporations, schools, and organizations and terms derived from those names to designate their members are capitalized. However, common nouns used descriptively or occurring after the names of two or more organizations are lowercased.

University of Michigan
Washington Huskies
played as a Pirate last year
Kiwanians
American and United airlines

The word *the* at the beginning of such names is capitalized only when the full legal name is used.

48. Words such as *agency, department, division, group,* or *office* that designate corporate and organizational units are capitalized only when they are used with a specific name.

> while working for the Criminal Division in the Department of Justice
> a notice to all department heads

Style varies regarding the capitalization of these words when they are used in place of the full name of a specific body; see paragraph 18 on pages 85–86.

49. Nicknames, epithets, or other alternative terms for organizations are capitalized.

> referred to IBM as Big Blue
> the Big Three automakers
> trading stocks on the Big Board

People

50. The names and initials of persons are capitalized. If a name is hyphenated, both elements are capitalized. Particles forming the initial elements of surnames (such as *de, della, der, du, la, ten, ter, van,* and *von*) may or may not be capitalized, depending on the practice of the family or individual. However, the particle is always capitalized at the beginning of a sentence.

E. I. du Pont de Nemours
James Van Allen
Sir Arthur Thomas Quiller-Couch
Wernher von Braun
the paintings of de Kooning
De Kooning's paintings are . . . .

51. The name of a person or thing can be added to or replaced entirely by a nickname or epithet (a characterizing word or phrase). Nicknames and epithets are capitalized.

Calamity Jane	Ol' Blue Eyes
Buffalo Bill	Attila the Hun
Magic Johnson	Meadowlark Lemon

52. Nicknames and epithets are frequently used in conjunction with both the first and last name of a person. If it is placed between the first and last name, it will often be enclosed in quotation marks or parentheses. However, if the nickname is in general use, the quotation marks or parentheses are often omitted. If the nickname precedes the first name, it is sometimes enclosed in quotation marks but more often not.

Earl ("Fatha") Hines
Joanne "Big Mama" Carner
Dennis (Oil Can) Boyd
Mother Maybelle Carter
Kissin' Jim Folsom

53. Words of family relationship preceding or used in place of a person's name are capital-

ized. However, these words are lowercased if
they are part of a noun phrase that is being
used in place of a name.

> Cousin Mercy
> Grandfather Barnes
> I know when Mother's birthday is.
> I know when my mother's birthday is.

54. Words designating languages, nationalities,
peoples, races, religious groups, and tribes
are capitalized. Descriptive terms used to
refer to groups of people are variously capitalized or lowercased. Designations based on
color are usually lowercased.

> Latino
> Caucasians
> Canadians
> African-American
> Muslims
> Ibo
> Bushman (nomadic hunter of southern Africa)
> bushman (inhabitant of the Australian bush)
> black, brown, and white people

55. Corporate, professional, and governmental
titles are capitalized when they immediately
precede a person's name, unless the name is
being used as an appositive.

> President Roosevelt
> Queen Elizabeth
> Doctor Malatesta
> Professor Kaiser
> Senator Sam Nunn

Pastor Linda Jones
the new pastor, Linda Jones
Chrysler's former president, Lee Iacocca

56. When corporate or governmental titles are used as part of a descriptive phrase to identify a person rather than as a person's official title, the title is lowercased.

Senator Bill Bradley of New Jersey
but
Bill Bradley, senator from New Jersey

Style varies when governmental titles are used in descriptive phrases that precede a name.

New Jersey senator Bill Bradley
or   New Jersey Senator Bill Bradley

57. Specific governmental titles may be capitalized when they are used in place of particular individuals' names. In minutes and official records of proceedings, corporate titles are capitalized when they are used in place of individuals' names.

The Secretary of State gave a news conference.
The Judge will respond to questions in her chambers.
The Treasurer then stated his misgivings about the project.

58. Some writers always capitalize the word *president* when it refers to the U.S. presidency. However, the more common practice is to capitalize the word *president* only when it refers to a specific individual.

> It is the duty of the president [President] to submit a budget to Congress.

59. Titles are capitalized when they are used in direct address.

> Tell me the truth, Doctor.
> Where are we headed, Captain?

Religious Terms

60. Words designating the Deity are capitalized.

Allah	Yahweh
Jehovah	the Creator
God Almighty	the Holy Spirit

61. Personal pronouns referring to the Deity are usually capitalized. Relative pronouns (such as *who*, *whom*, and *whose*) usually are not.

> God in His mercy
> believing that it was God who created the universe

62. Traditional designations of apostles, prophets, and saints are capitalized.

> our Lady
> the Prophet
> the Lawgiver

63. Names of religions, denominations, creeds and confessions, and religious orders are capitalized, as are adjectives derived from these

names. The word *church* is capitalized only
when it is used as part of the name of a specific body or edifice or, in some publications,
when it refers to organized Christianity in
general.

Judaism
the Southern Baptist Convention
Apostles' Creed
the Poor Clares
the Society of Jesus
Islamic
Hunt Memorial Church
the Baptist church on the corner

64. Names of the Bible or its books, parts, ver-
sions, or editions of it and other sacred books
are capitalized but not italicized. Adjectives
derived from the names of sacred books are
variously capitalized and lowercased. When
in doubt, consult a dictionary.

Gospel of Saint Mark	Talmud
Old Testament	Talmudic
Authorized Version	Koran
biblical	Koranic

65. The names of prayers and well-known passages of the Bible are capitalized.

the Ave Maria
the Lord's Prayer
the Our Father
the Ten Commandments
the Sermon on the Mount
the Beatitudes

Scientific Terms

66. Genus names in biological binomial nomenclature are capitalized; species names are lowercased, even when derived from a proper name. Both genus and species names are italicized.

> Both the wolf and the domestic dog are included in the genus *Canis*.
> The California condor (*Gymnogyps californianus*) is facing extinction.

The names of races, varieties, or subspecies, when used, are lowercased. Like genus and species names, they are italicized.

> *Hyla versicolor chrysoscelis*
> *Otis asio naevius*

67. The New Latin names of classes, families, and all groups above the genus level in zoology and botany are capitalized but not italicized. Their derivative adjectives and nouns in English are neither capitalized nor italicized.

> Gastropoda   gastropod
> Thallophyta   thallophyte

68. The names, both scientific and informal, of planets and their satellites, asteroids, stars, constellations, groups of stars, and other specific celestial objects are capitalized. However, the words *sun, earth,* and *moon* are usually lowercased unless they occur with other astronomical names. A generic term that follows the name of a celestial object is usually lowercased.

the Milky Way	Big Dipper
Pleiades	the Moon and Mars
Sirius	Barnard's star

69. Names of meteorological phenomena are lowercased.

aurora borealis
northern lights
parhelic circle

70. Terms that identify geological eras, periods, epochs, and strata are capitalized. The generic terms that follow them are lowercased. The words *upper, middle,* and *lower* are capitalized when they are used to designate an epoch or series within a period; in most other cases, they are lowercased. The word *age* is capitalized in names such as *Age of Reptiles* or *Age of Fishes.*

Mesozoic era
Upper Cretaceous
Quaternary period
Middle Ordovician
Oligocene epoch
Lower Silurian

71. Proper names forming essential elements of scientific laws, theorems, and principles are capitalized. However, the common nouns *law, theorem, theory,* and the like are lowercased.

> Boyle's law
> the Pythagorean theorem
> Planck's constant
> Einstein's theory of relativity

In terms referring to popular or fanciful theories or observations, descriptive words are usually capitalized as well.

> Murphy's Law
> the Peter Principle

72. The names of chemical elements and compounds are lowercased.

> hydrogen fluoride
> ferric ammonium citrate

73. The names of computer services and databases are usually trademarks and should always be capitalized. Some names of computer languages are written with an initial capital letter, some with all letters capitalized. Some are commonly written both ways. When in doubt, consult a dictionary.

CompuServe	PL/1
Atek	APL
BASIC	PASCAL *or* Pascal
TeleTransfer	COBOL *or* Cobol

Time Periods and Zones

74. The names of the days of the week, months of the year, and holidays and holy days are capitalized.

Tuesday	Thanksgiving
June	Easter
Independence Day	Yom Kippur

75. The names of time zones are capitalized when abbreviated but usually lowercased when written out, except for words that are themselves proper names.

CST	mountain time
central standard time	Pacific standard time

76. Names of the seasons are lowercased if they simply declare the time of year; however, they are capitalized if they are personified.

> My new book is scheduled to appear this spring.
> the sweet breath of Spring

Titles

77. Words in titles of books, long poems, magazines, newspapers, plays, movies, novellas that are separately published, and works of art such as paintings and sculpture are capitalized except for internal articles, conjunctions, prepositions, and the *to* of infinitives. (Some writers also capitalize prepositions of five or more letters such as *about* or *toward*.) The entire title is italicized. Regarding the Bible and other sacred works, see paragraph 64 on page 100.

> *The Lives of a Cell*
> *Of Mice and Men*
> *National Geographic*

Christian Science Monitor
Shakespeare's *Othello*
the movie *Wait until Dark*
Géricault's *The Raft of the Medusa*

78. An initial article that is part of a title is often omitted if it would be awkward in context. However, when it is included it is capitalized and italicized or underlined. For books that are referred to by an abbreviation, the initial article is neither capitalized nor italicized.

The Oxford English Dictionary
the 20-volume *Oxford English Dictionary*
the *OED*

79. Practice varies widely regarding the capitalization and italicization or underlining of initial articles and city names in the titles of newspapers. The most common practice is to italicize the city name but not to capitalize or italicize the initial article.

the *New York Times*
the *Wall Street Journal*

80. Many publications, especially newspapers, do not use italics for titles. They either simply capitalize the words of the title or capitalize the words and enclose them in quotation marks.

the Heard on the Street column in the Wall Street Journal
our review of "The Volcano Lover" in last week's issue

81. The first word following a colon in a title is capitalized.

> *Jane Austen: A Literary Life*

82. The titles of short poems, short stories, essays, lectures, dissertations, chapters of books, articles in periodicals, radio and television programs, and novellas that are published in a collection are capitalized and enclosed in quotation marks. The capitalization of articles, conjunctions, and prepositions is the same as it is for italicized titles, as explained in paragraph 77 above.

> Robert Frost's "Dust of Snow"
> Cynthia Ozick's "Rosa"
> John Barth's "The Literature of Exhaustion"
> The talk, "Labor's Power: A View for the Nineties," will be given Friday.
> the third chapter of *Treasure Island,* entitled "The Black Spot"
> Her article, "Computer Art on a Micro," was in *Popular Computing.*
> listening to "All Things Considered"
> watching "The Tonight Show"

83. Common titles of book sections (such as *preface, introduction,* or *index*) are capitalized but not enclosed in quotation marks when they refer to a section of the same book in which the reference is made. If they refer to another book, they are usually lowercased.

> See the Appendix for further information.
> In the introduction to her book, the author explains her goals.

84. Practice varies regarding the capitalization of the word *chapter* when it is used with a cardinal number to identify a specific chapter in a book. Most writers capitalize the word, but some do not.

> See Chapter 3 for more details.
> is discussed further in Chapter Four
> > *but*
> in the third chapter

85. The titles of long musical compositions are generally capitalized and italicized; the titles of songs and other short compositions are capitalized and enclosed in quotation marks. The titles of compositions identified only by the nature of the musical form in which they were written are capitalized only, regardless of their length.

> Verdi's *Don Carlos*
> Beethoven's "Für Elise"
> "America the Beautiful"
> Symphony No. 8 in F Major

Trademarks

86. Registered trademarks, service marks, collective marks, and brand names are capitalized.

Band-Aid	Velcro
College Board	Diet Pepsi
Kellogg's All-Bran	Kleenex
Jacuzzi	Lay's potato chips

Transportation

87. The names of individual ships, submarines, airplanes, satellites, and space vehicles are capitalized and italicized. The designations *U.S.S.*, *S.S.*, *M.V.*, and *H.M.S.* are not italicized.

Apollo 11	*Enola Gay*
Spirit of St. Louis	M.V. *West Star*

Other Uses of Capitals

1. Full capitalization of a word is sometimes used for emphasis or to indicate that a speaker is talking very loudly. Both of these uses of capitals are usually avoided in formal writing. Italicizing words for emphasis is more common (for examples, see paragraph 7 on page 112).

> Results are not the only criteria for judging performance. HOW we achieve results is important also.
>
> All applications must be submitted IN WRITING before January 31.
>
> The waiter rushed by yelling "HOT PLATE! HOT PLATE!"

2. A word is sometimes capitalized to indicate that it is being used as a philosophical concept or that it stands for an important concept in a discussion.

> Many people seek Truth, but few find it.
> the three M's of advertising: Message, Media, and Management

3. Full capitals or a mixture of capitals and lowercase letters or sometimes even small capitals are used to reproduce the text of signs, labels, or inscriptions.

> a poster reading SPECIAL THRILLS COMING SOON
> a Do Not Disturb sign
> a barn with CHEW MAIL POUCH on the side

4. A letter used to indicate a shape is capitalized.

> an A-frame house
> a J-bar
> V-shaped

Other Uses of Italics

For each of the uses listed below, italic type is used in keyboarded or typeset material (or where it is otherwise available); in typed or handwritten material, underlining is used.

1. Foreign words and phrases that have not been fully adopted into the English language are italicized. The decision whether or not to italicize a word will vary according to context and the audience for which the writing is intended. In general, however, any word that appears in the main A–Z vocabulary section of *Merriam-Webster's Collegiate Dictionary, Tenth Edition* does not need to be italicized.

> These accomplishments will serve as a monument, *aere perennius,* to the group's skill and dedication.
>
> "The cooking here is *wunderbar,*" he said.
>
> After the concert, the crowd headed en masse for the parking lot.
>
> The committee meets on an ad hoc basis.

A complete sentence (such as a motto) can also be italicized. However, passages that consist of more than one sentence, or even a single sentence if it is particularly long, are usually treated as quotations; that is, they are set in roman type and enclosed in quotation marks.

2. Unfamiliar words or words that have a specialized meaning are set in italics, especially when they are accompanied by a short definition. Once these words have been introduced and defined, they do not need to be italicized in subsequent references.

> *Vitiligo* is a condition in which skin pigment cells stop making pigment.
>
> Another method is the *direct-to-consumer* transaction, in which the publisher markets directly to the individual by mail or door-to-door.

3. Latin abbreviations are usually not italicized, although the traditional practice has been to italicize them, and some writers still do so.

et al.	i.e.
cf.	viz.

4. Italic type is used to indicate words referred to as words, letters referred to as letters, or numerals referred to as numerals. However, if the word referred to as a word was actually spoken, it is often enclosed in quotation marks. If the letter is being used to refer to its sound and not its printed form, slashes or brackets can be used instead of italics. And if there is no chance of confusion, numerals referred to as numerals are often not italicized. (For plurals of words, letters, and numerals referred to as such, see paragraphs 17–19 and 25 on pages 120 and 122.)

> The panel could not decide whether *data* was a singular or plural noun.
>
> *Only* can be an adverb, as in the case of "I *only* tried to help."
>
> We heard his warning, but we weren't sure what "other repercussions" meant in that context.
>
> You should dot your *i*'s and cross your *t*'s.
>
> He was still having trouble with the /p/ sound.
>
> The first *2* and the last *1* are barely legible.

A letter used to indicate a shape is capitalized but not set in italics (for examples, see paragraph 4 on page 109).

5. Individual letters are sometimes set in italic type to provide additional typographical contrast. This use of italics is common when letters are used in enumerations within sentences or when they are used to identify elements in an illustration.

> providing information about *(a)* typing, *(b)* transcribing, *(c)* formatting, and *(d)* graphics
>
> located at point *A* on the diagram

6. Italics are used to indicate a word created to suggest a sound.

> We sat listening to the *chat-chat-chat* of the sonar.

7. Italics are used to emphasize or draw attention to a word or words in a sentence.

> Students must notify the dean's office *in writing* of all courses added to or dropped from their original list.
>
> She had become *the* hero, the one everyone else looked up to.

Italics serve to draw attention to words in large part because they are used so infrequently. The overuse of italics may cause them to lose their effectiveness.

Chapter 3

Plurals, Possessives, and Compounds

This chapter describes the ways in which plurals, possessives, and compounds are most commonly formed. For some of the questions treated here, various solutions have been developed over the years but no single solution has come to be universally accepted. In these cases, the range of available solutions is described and you must use your own judgment to choose among them.

In regard to plurals, consulting a good dictionary will solve many of the problems that are discussed in this chapter. The best dictionary to consult is an unabridged dictionary, such as *Webster's Third New International Dictionary*. The next best is a good college dictionary, such as *Merriam-Webster's Collegiate Dictionary, Tenth Edition*. Any dictionary that is much smaller than the *Collegiate* will often be more frustrating in what it fails to show than helpful in what it shows.

In giving examples of plurals, possessives, and compounds, this chapter uses both *or* and *also* to separate variant forms of the same word. The word *or* is used when both forms of the word are used with approximately equal frequency in standard writing; the first form is probably slightly more common than the second. The word *also* is used when the first form of the word is much more common than the second.

Plurals

The plurals of most English words are formed by adding *-s* to the singular. If the noun ends in *-s*, *-x*, *-z*, *-ch*, or *-sh*, so that an extra syllable must be added in order to pronounce the plural, *-es* is added to the singular. If the noun ends in a *-y* preceded by a consonant, the *-y* is changed to *-i-* and *-es* is added.

However, many English nouns do not follow this general pattern. Most good dictionaries give thorough coverage to irregular and variant plurals, so they are often the best place to start to answer questions about the plural form of a specific word. The paragraphs that follow describe how plurals are formed for a number of categories of words whose plural forms are most apt to raise questions. The symbol → is used here to link the singular and plural forms.

Abbreviations

1. The plurals of abbreviations are commonly formed by adding *-s* or an apostrophe plus *-s*; however, there are some significant excep-

tions. (For more on forming plurals of abbreviations, see paragraphs 1–5 on pages 157–58.)

COLA → COLAs   Ph.D. → Ph.D.'s
f.o.b. → f.o.b.'s   bldg. → bldgs.
CPU → CPUs   p. → pp.

Animals

2. The names of many fishes, birds, and mammals have both a plural formed with a suffix and one that is identical with the singular. Some have only one or the other.

flounder → flounder *or* flounders
quail → quail *or* quails
mink → mink *or* minks
caribou → caribou *or* caribous
rat → rats
monkey → monkeys
moose → moose

3. Many of the animals that have both plural forms are ones that are hunted, fished, or trapped; those who hunt, fish for, and trap them are most likely to use the unchanged form. The *-s* form is often used to emphasize diversity of kinds.

caught four trout
    but
trouts of the Rocky Mountains
a place where fish gather
    but
the fishes of the Pacific Ocean

Compounds and Phrases

4. Most compounds made up of two nouns—
whether they appear as one word, two words,
or a hyphenated word—form their plurals
by pluralizing the final element only.

> matchbox → matchboxes
> judge advocate → judge advocates
> city-state → city-states
> crow's-foot → crow's-feet

5. The plural form of a compound consisting of
an -*er* noun and an adverb is made by pluralizing the noun element only.

> hanger-on → hangers-on
> onlooker → onlookers
> looker-on → lookers-on
> passerby → passersby

6. Nouns made up of words that are not nouns
form their plurals on the last element.

> also-ran → also-rans
> put-down → put-downs
> changeover → changeovers
> ne'er-do-well → ne'er-do-wells
> set-to → set-tos
> blowup → blowups

7. Plurals of compounds that are phrases consisting of two nouns separated by a preposition are regularly formed by pluralizing the
first noun.

> aide-de-camp → aides-de-camp
> attorney-at-law → attorneys-at-law

power of attorney → powers of attorney
base on balls → bases on balls
man-of-war → men-of-war
coup d'état → coups d'état

8. Compounds that are phrases consisting of two nouns separated by a preposition and a modifier form their plurals in various ways.

flash in the pan → flashes in the pan
jack-in-the-box → jack-in-the-boxes
     or jacks-in-the-box
jack-of-all-trades → jacks-of-all-trades
stick-in-the-mud → stick-in-the-muds

9. Compounds consisting of a noun followed by an adjective are usually pluralized by adding -*s* or -*es* to the noun.

cousin-german → cousins-german
heir apparent → heirs apparent
knight-errant → knights-errant

If the adjective in such a compound tends to be construed as a noun, the compound may have more than one plural form.

attorney general → attorneys general
     or attorney generals
sergeant major → sergeants major
     or sergeant majors
poet laureate → poets laureate *or* poet laureates

Foreign Words and Phrases

10. Many nouns of foreign origin retain the foreign plural. However, most of them also have a regular English plural.

alumnus → alumni
beau → beaux *or* beaus
crisis → crises
index → indexes *or* indices
phenomenon → phenomena *or* phenomenons
schema → schemata *also* schemas
series → series
tempo → tempi *or* tempos

A foreign plural may not be used for all senses of a word, or may be more commonly used for some senses than for others.

antenna (on an insect) → antennae
antenna (on a radio) → antennas

11. Phrases of foreign origin may have a foreign plural, an English plural, or both.

carte blanche → cartes blanches
hors d'oeuvre → hors d'oeuvres
beau monde → beau mondes
　　　　　　or beaux mondes

Words Ending in *-ful*

12. A plural *-fuls* can be used for any noun ending in *-ful*, but some of these nouns also have an alternative plural with *-s-* preceding the suffix.

eyeful → eyefuls
bucketful → bucketfuls *or* bucketsful
cupful → cupfuls *also* cupsful

Irregular Plurals

13. A small group of English nouns form their plurals by changing one or more of their vowels.

foot → feet

goose → geese

louse → lice

man → men

mouse → mice

woman → women

tooth → teeth

14. A few nouns have *-en* or *-ren* plurals.

ox → oxen

child → children

brother → brethren

15. Some nouns ending in *-f*, *-fe*, and *-ff* have plurals that end in *-ves*. Some of these also have regularly formed plurals.

elf → elves

knife → knives

life → lives

beef → beefs *or* beeves

staff → staffs *or* staves

wharf → wharves *also* wharfs

Italic Elements

16. Italicized words, phrases, abbreviations, and letters may be pluralized with either an italic or, more commonly, a roman *s*. If the plural is formed with an apostrophe and an *-s*, the *-s* is almost always roman.

fifteen *Newsweek*s on the shelf
answered with a series of *uh-huhs*
a row of *x*'s

Letters

17. The plurals of letters are usually formed by
adding an apostrophe and an *-s,* although
capital letters are sometimes pluralized by
adding an *-s* alone.

p's and q's
V's of geese flying overhead
dot your *i*'s
straight As

Numbers

18. Numerals are pluralized by adding an *-s* or,
less commonly, an apostrophe and an *-s.*

two par 5s *or* two par 5's
1970s *or* 1970's
in the 80s *or* in the 80's
the mid-$20,000s *or* the mid-$20,000's

19. Spelled-out numbers are usually pluralized
without an apostrophe.

in twos and threes
scored two sixes

Words Ending in *-o*

20. Most words ending in *-o* are pluralized by
adding an *-s.* However, some words ending
in *-o* preceded by a consonant take *-es* plurals,
and some may take either *-s* or *-es.* When in
doubt, consult a dictionary.

alto → altos
echo → echoes *also* echos
motto → mottoes *also* mottos

Proper Nouns

21. The plurals of proper nouns are usually formed with -*s* or -*es*.

Bruce → Bruces
Hastings → Hastingses
Velázquez → Velázquezes

22. Proper nouns ending in -*y* usually retain the -*y* and add -*s*.

February → Februarys
Marys → Marys
Mercury → Mercurys
  but
Ptolemy → Ptolemies
Sicily → The Two Sicilies
The Rockies

Words that were originally proper nouns and that end in -*y* are usually pluralized by changing -*y* to -*i* and adding -*es*, but a few retain the -*y*.

bobby → bobbies
Jerry → Jerries
johnny → johnnies
Tommy → Tommies
Bloody Mary → Bloody Marys

Quoted Elements

23. Practice varies regarding the plural form of words in quotation marks. Some writers form the plural by adding an -*s* or an apostrophe plus -*s* within the quotation marks. Others add an -*s* outside the quotation marks. Both arrangements look awkward, and writers generally try to avoid this construction.

> too many "probably's" in the statement
> one "you" among millions of "you"s
> a response characterized by its "yes, but"s

Symbols

24. Symbols are not usually pluralized except when being referred to as characters in themselves, without regard to meaning. The plural is formed by adding an -*s* or an apostrophe plus -*s*.

> used &'s instead of *and*'s
> his π's are hard to read
> printed three *s

Words Used as Words

25. Words used as words without regard to meaning usually form their plurals by adding an apostrophe and a roman -*s*.

> five *and*'s in one sentence
> all those *wherefore*'s and *howsoever*'s

When a word used as a word has become part of a fixed phrase, the plural is usually formed by adding a roman -*s* without the apostrophe.

> oohs and aahs
> dos and don'ts   *or*   do's and don't's

Possessives

The possessive case of most nouns is formed by adding an apostrophe or an apostrophe plus -*s* to the end of the word.

Common Nouns

1. The possessive case of singular and plural common nouns that do not end in an *s* or *z* sound is formed by adding an apostrophe plus -*s* to the end of the word.

   the boy's mother   children's books
   men's clothing   the potato's skin
   her dog's leash   the essay's theme

2. The possessive case of singular nouns ending in an *s* or *z* sound is usually formed by adding an apostrophe plus -*s* to the end of the word. An alternative approach, although one less widely accepted, is to add an apostrophe plus -*s* to the word only when the added -*s* is easily pronounced; if adding the -*s* is felt to create a word that is difficult to pronounce, only an apostrophe is added.

   the press's books
   the boss's desk
   the index's arrangement
   the horse's saddle
   the princess's duties   *also*   the princess' duties

Even those who follow the pattern of adding an apostrophe plus -*s* to all singular nouns will often make an exception for a multisyllabic word that ends in an *s* or *z* sound if it is followed by a word beginning with an *s* or *z* sound.

> for convenience' sake
> for conscience' sake

3. The possessive case of plural nouns ending in an *s* or *z* sound is formed by adding only an apostrophe to the end of the word. One exception to this rule is that the possessive case of one-syllable irregular plurals is usually formed by adding an apostrophe plus *-s*.

> horses' stalls
> geese's calls
> consumers' confidence
> mice's habits

Proper Names

4. The possessive forms of proper names are generally made in the same way as they are for common nouns. The possessive form of singular proper names not ending in an *s* or *z* sound is made by adding an apostrophe plus *-s* to the name. The possessive form of plural proper names is made by adding just an apostrophe.

> Mrs. Wilson's store
> the Wattses' daughter
> Utah's capital
> the Cohens' house
> Canada's rivers
> Niagara Falls' location

5. As is the case for the possessive form of singular common nouns (see paragraph 2 above), the possessive form of singular proper names ending in an *s* or *z* sound may be formed either by adding an apostrophe plus -*s* or by adding just an apostrophe to the name. For the sake of consistency, most writers choose one pattern for forming the possessive of all singular names ending in an *s* or *z* sound, regardless of the pronunciation of individual names (for exceptions see paragraphs 6 and 7 below). Adding an apostrophe plus -*s* to all such names is more common than adding just the apostrophe.

> Jones's car *also* Jones' car
> Bliss's statue *also* Bliss' statue
> Dickens's novels *also* Dickens' novels

6. The possessive form of classical and biblical names of two or more syllables ending in -*s* or -*es* is usually made by adding an apostrophe without an -*s*. If the name has only one syllable, the possessive form is made by adding an apostrophe and an -*s*.

> Aristophanes' plays   Judas' betrayal
> Achilles' heel   Zeus's anger
> Odysseus' journey   Mars's help

7. The possessive forms of the names *Jesus* and *Moses* are always formed with just an apostrophe.

> Jesus' time
> Moses' law

8. The possessive forms of names ending in a silent *-s*, *-z*, or *-x* usually include the apostrophe and the *-s*.

> Arkansas's capital
> Camus's *The Stranger*
> Josquin des Prez's music
> Delacroix's painting

9. When the possessive ending is added to a name that is in italics, it is usually not italicized.

> the U.S.S. *Constitution*'s cannons
> *Gone with the Wind*'s ending
> the *Mona Lisa*'s somber hues
> *High Noon*'s plot

Pronouns

10. The possessive case of indefinite pronouns such as *anyone, everybody,* and *someone* is formed by adding an apostrophe and an *-s*.

> anyone's   someone's
> everybody's   somebody's

Some indefinite pronouns usually require an *of* phrase to indicate possession.

> the rights of each
> the inclination of many
> the satisfaction of all

11. Possessive pronouns do not include apostrophes.

mine	hers
ours	his
yours	theirs
its	

Phrases

12. The possessive form of a phrase is made by adding an apostrophe or an apostrophe plus -*s* to the last word in the phrase.

> board of directors' meeting
> his brother-in-law's sidecar
> from the student of politics' point of view
> after a moment or so's thought

Constructions such as these can become awkward, and it is often better to rephrase the sentence to eliminate the need for the possessive ending. For instance, the last two examples above could be rephrased as follows:

> from the point of view of the student of politics
> after thinking for a moment or so

Words in Quotation Marks

13. The possessive form of words in quotation marks can be formed in two ways, with the apostrophe plus -*s* placed either inside the quotation marks or outside them. Both arrangements look awkward, and this construction is best avoided.

> the "Today Show" 's cohosts
> the "Grande Dame's" escort
> *but more commonly*

the cohosts of the "Today Show"
escort to the "Grande Dame"

Abbreviations

14. Possessives of abbreviations are formed like those of nouns that are spelled out. The singular possessive is formed by adding an apostrophe plus *-s* to the abbreviation; the plural possessive, by adding an apostrophe only.

the AMA's executive committee
Itek Corp.'s Applied Technology Division
the MPs' decisions

Numerals

15. The possessive form of nouns composed of numerals is made in the same way as for other nouns. The possessive of singular nouns is formed by adding an apostrophe plus *-s*; the possessive form of plural nouns is formed by adding an apostrophe only.

1995's most popular model
the 1980s' most colorful figure

Individual and Joint Possession

16. Individual possession is indicated by adding an apostrophe plus *-s* to each noun in a sequence. Joint possession is most commonly indicated by adding an apostrophe or an apostrophe plus *-s* to the last noun in the sequence, but may also be indicated by adding a possessive ending to each name.

Kepler's and Clark's respective clients
John's, Bill's, and Larry's boats
Bissell and Hansen's law firm
Christine and James's vacation home
   or   Christine's and James's vacation home

Compounds

A compound is a word or word group that consists of two or more parts that work together as a unit to express a specific concept. Compounds can be formed by combining two or more words (as in *eye shadow, graphic equalizer, farmhouse, cost-effective, blue-pencil, around-the-clock,* or *son of a gun*), by combining prefixes or suffixes with words (as in *ex-president, shoeless, presorted, uninterruptedly,* or *meaningless*), or by combining two or more word elements (as in *supermicro* or *photomicrograph*). Compounds are written in one of three ways: solid (as in *cottonmouth*), hyphenated (*player-manager*), or open (*field day*).

Permanent compounds are compounds that are so commonly used that they have become permanent parts of the language; many of them are entered in dictionaries. *Temporary compounds* are those created to fit a writer's need at a particular moment (such as *quasi government*); thus, they cannot be found in dictionaries. *Self-evident compounds* are compounds that are readily understood from the meanings of the words that make them up (such as *baseball game* or *economic policy*).

Most self-evident compounds are not entered in dictionaries. Writers thus cannot rely wholly on dictionaries to guide them in writing compounds, but must develop an approach for dealing with those that are not in the dictionary.

One approach is simply to leave open any compound that is not in the dictionary. Many writers do this, but there are drawbacks to this approach. A temporary compound may not be easily recognized as a compound when it is left open. For instance, if you need to use *wide body* as a term for a kind of jet airplane, a phrase like "the operation of wide bodies" may catch the reader unawares. And if you use the open style for a compound modifier, you may create momentary confusion (or even unintended amusement) with a phrase like "the operation of wide body jets."

Another possibility is to hyphenate all compounds not in the dictionary. Hyphenation gives your compound immediate recognition as a compound. But hyphenating all such compounds runs counter to some well-established American practice, and might thus call too much attention to the compound and momentarily distract the reader.

A third approach is to pattern your temporary compound after some other similar compound. This approach is likely to be more complicated, and usually will not free you from the need to make your own decisions. But it does have the advantage of making your compound less distracting or confusing by making it look like other more familiar compounds. The paragraphs that follow are aimed at helping you to use this third approach.

The symbol + in the following paragraphs can be interpreted as "followed immediately by."

Compound Nouns

Compound nouns are combinations of words that function in a sentence as nouns. They may consist of two or more nouns, a noun and a modifier, or two or more elements that are not nouns.

1. **noun + noun** Compounds composed of two nouns that are short, commonly used, and pronounced with falling stress—that is, with the most stress on the first noun and less or no stress on the second—are usually written solid.

teapot	birdbath
catfish	handsaw
cottonmouth	handmaiden
sweatband	farmyard

2. When a noun + noun compound is short and common but pronounced with nearly equal stress on both nouns, it is more likely to be open.

bean sprouts	beach buggy
fuel oil	duffel bag

3. Many short noun + noun compounds begin as temporary compounds written open. As

they become more familiar and better established, there is a tendency for them to become solid.

data base *has become* database
chain saw *is becoming* chainsaw
lawn mower *is becoming* lawnmower

4. Noun + noun compounds that consist of longer nouns and are self-evident or temporary are usually written open.

wildlife sanctuary
football game
television camera
reunion dinner

5. When the nouns in a noun + noun compound describe a double title or double function, the compound is hyphenated.

city-state	secretary-treasurer
decree-law	player-manager
dinner-dance	author-critic

6. Compounds formed from a noun or adjective followed by *man, woman, person,* or *people* and denoting an occupation are normally solid.

salesman	salesperson
congresswoman	spokesperson
handyman	salespeople

7. Compounds that are units of measurement are hyphenated.

foot-pound	column-inch
kilowatt-hour	light-year

8. adjective + noun   Most adjective + noun compounds are written open.

automatic weapons	minor seminary
religious freedom	modular arithmetic
pancreatic juice	graphic equalizer

9. Adjective + noun compounds consisting of two short words may be written solid when pronounced with falling stress. However, short adjective + noun compounds are often written open; a few are hyphenated.

shortcut	dry run
longhand	long haul
blueprint	red tape
drywall	yellow jacket
wetland	red-eye

10. participle + noun   Most participle + noun compounds are written open.

running total
whipped cream
furnished apartment
nagging backache
shredded wheat

11. noun's + noun   Compounds consisting of a possessive noun followed by another noun are usually written hyphenated or open.

crow's-feet	hornet's nest
cat's-paw	lion's share
cat's cradle	fool's gold

Compounds of this type that have become solid have lost the apostrophe.

foolscap
menswear
sheepshead

12. **noun + verb + -er; noun + verb + -ing** Temporary or self-evident compounds in which the first noun is the object of the verb to which the suffix has been added are most often written open. However, a hyphen may be used to make the relationships of the words immediately apparent. Permanent compounds like these are sometimes written solid as well.

temporary or		
self-evident:	opinion seeker	cost-cutter
	career planning	risk-taking
permanent:	data processing	bookkeeper
	bird-watcher	lifesaver
	fund-raising	copyediting

13. **object + verb** Noun compounds consisting of a verb preceded by a noun that is its object are written in various ways.

clambake	face-lift
car wash	turkey shoot

14. **verb + object** A few, mostly older compounds are formed from a verb followed by a noun that is its object; they are written solid.

tosspot	carryall
cutthroat	pinchpenny
breakwater	pickpocket

15. **noun + adjective**   Compounds composed of a noun followed by an adjective are written open or hyphenated.

battle royal	heir apparent
sum total	president-elect
consul general	secretary-general

16. **particle + noun**   Compounds consisting of a particle (usually a preposition or adverb) and a noun are usually written solid, especially when they are short and pronounced with falling stress.

downpour	undershirt
output	outpatient
offshoot	aftershock
inpatient	upkeep

A few particle + noun compounds, especially when composed of longer elements or having equal stress on both elements, may be hyphenated or open.

off-season	off year
cross-fertilization	down payment

17. **verb + particle; verb + adverb**   These compounds may be hyphenated or solid. Compounds with two-letter particles (*by, to, in, up, on*) are usually hyphenated, since the hyphen aids quick comprehension. Compounds with three-letter particles (*off, out*) are hyphenated

or solid with about equal frequency. Those with longer particles or adverbs are more often solid.

flyby	turnoff
set-to	shoot-out
sit-in	dropout
letup	breakthrough
run-on	giveaway
show-off	gadabout

18. verb + -*er* + particle; verb + -*ing* + particle   Except for *passerby*, these compounds are hyphenated.

hanger-on	talking-to
runner-up	falling-out
looker-on	goings-on

19. Compounds of three or four elements   Compounds of three or four elements may be either hyphenated or open. Those consisting of noun + prepositional phrase are generally open, although some are hyphenated. Those formed from other combinations are usually hyphenated.

base on balls	jack-of-all-trades
lily of the valley	know-it-all
justice of the peace	pick-me-up

20. letter + noun   Compounds formed from a single letter (or sometimes a combination of them) followed by a noun are either open or hyphenated.

A-frame	Rh factor
C ration	T-shirt
D day	T square
H-bomb	H and L hinge

Compounds That Function as Adjectives

Compound adjectives are combinations of words that work together to modify a noun—that is, they work as *unit modifiers*. As unit modifiers they should be distinguished from other strings of adjectives that may also precede a noun.

For instance, in "a low, level tract of land" or "that long, lonesome road" the two adjectives each modify the noun separately. We are talking about a tract of land that is both low and level and about a road that is both long and lonesome. These are *coordinate modifiers*.

In "a low monthly fee" or "suggested retail price" the first adjective modifies the noun plus the second adjective. In other words, we mean a monthly fee that is low and the retail price that has been suggested. These are *noncoordinate modifiers*.

But in "low-level radiation" we do not mean radiation that is low and level or level radiation that is low; we mean radiation that is at a low level. Both words work as a unit to modify the noun. Unit modifiers are usually hyphenated. The hyphens not only make it easier for the readers to grasp the relationship of the words but also avoid confusion. The hyphen in "a call for more-specialized controls" removes any ambiguity as to which word *more* modifies. By contrast, the lack of a hyphen in a phrase like "graphic arts exhibition" may give it an undesirable ambiguity.

21. **Before the noun (attributive position)** Most two-word permanent or temporary compound adjectives are hyphenated when placed before the noun.

> tree-lined streets
> well-intended advice
> a trumped-up charge
> fast-acting medication
> an input-output device
> a risk-free investment

22. Temporary or self-evident compounds formed of an adverb (such as *well, more, less, still*) followed by a participle (or sometimes an adjective) are usually hyphenated when placed before a noun.

> a well-funded project
> more-specialized controls
> a still-growing company
> these fast-moving times
> a just-completed survey
> a now-vulnerable politician

23. Compounds formed from an adverb ending in *-ly* followed by a participle may sometimes be hyphenated but are more commonly open, because adverb + adjective + noun is a normal word order.

a widely-read feature
internationally-known authors
but more often
a widely read feature
internationally known authors

24. The combination of *very* + adjective is not a unit modifier.

a very satisfied smile

25. Many compound adjectives are formed by using a compound noun—either permanent or temporary—to modify another noun. If the compound noun is an open compound, it is usually hyphenated to make the relationship of the words more immediately apparent.

the farm-bloc vote
a tax-law case
a picture-framing shop
a secret-compartment ring
ocean-floor hydrophones

26. Some open compound nouns are so recognizable that they are frequently placed before a noun without a hyphen.

a high school diploma
or a high-school diploma
a data processing course
or a data-processing course
a dry goods store *or* a dry-goods store

27. A proper name placed before a noun to modify it is not hyphenated.

> a Thames River marina
> a Korean War veteran
> a Huck Finn life
> a General Motors car

28. Compound adjectives of three or more words are hyphenated when they precede the noun. Many temporary compounds are formed by hyphenating a phrase and placing it before a noun.

> spur-of-the-moment decisions
> higher-than-anticipated costs

29. Compound adjectives composed of foreign words are not hyphenated when placed before a noun unless they are hyphenated in the foreign language itself.

> the per capita cost
> a cordon bleu restaurant
> an a priori argument
> a ci-devant professor

30. Chemical names used as modifiers before a noun are not hyphenated.

> a sodium hypochlorite bleach
> a citric acid solution

31. Following the noun (as a complement or predicate adjective) When the words that make up a compound adjective follow the noun they modify, they tend to fall in normal word order and are no longer unit modifiers. They are therefore no longer hyphenated.

> arrested on charges that had been trumped up
> decisions made on the spur of the moment
> They were ill prepared for the journey.

32. Many permanent and temporary compounds keep their hyphens after the noun in a sentence if they continue to function as unit modifiers.

> Your ideas are high-minded but impractical.
> You were just as nice-looking then.
> metals that are corrosion-resistant
> tends to be accident-prone

33. Permanent compound adjectives are usually written as they appear in the dictionary, whether they precede or follow the noun they modify.

> The group was public-spirited.
> The problems are mind-boggling.
> is well-read in economics

34. Compound adjectives of three or more words are normally not hyphenated when they follow the noun they modify.

> These remarks are off the record.

35. Permanent compounds of three or more words may appear as hyphenated adjectives in dictionaries. In such cases the hyphens are retained as long as the phrase is being used as a unit modifier.

the plan is still pay-as-you-go
but   a plan in which you pay as you go

36. It is possible that a permanent hyphenated
adjective may appear alongside a temporary
compound in a position where it would normally be open (such as "one who is both ill-
humored and ill prepared"). In such cases, it
is best to either hyphenate both compounds
or leave both open.

37. When an adverb modifies another adverb
that is the first element of a compound modifier, the compound may lose its hyphen. If
the first adverb modifies the whole compound, however, the hyphen should be retained.

a very well developed idea
a delightfully well-written book
a most ill-humored remark

38. Adjective compounds that are names of
colors may be written open or hyphenated.
Color names in which each element can function as a noun (such as *blue green* or *chrome yellow*) are almost always hyphenated when they
precede a noun; they are sometimes open
when they follow the noun. Color names in
which the first element can only be an adjective are often not hyphenated before a noun
and usually not hyphenated after.

blue-gray paint
paint that is blue-gray

also   paint that is blue gray
bluish gray paint   *or*   bluish-gray paint

39. Compound modifiers that include a number followed by a noun are hyphenated when they precede the noun they modify. When the modifier follows the noun, it is usually not hyphenated.

five-card stud
10-foot pole
12-year-old girl
a child who is seven years old
an 18-inch rule   *but*   a 10 percent raise

40. An adjective that is composed of a number followed by a noun in the possessive is not hyphenated.

a two weeks' wait
a nine days' wonder

Compounds That Function as Adverbs

41. Adverb compounds consisting of preposition + noun are almost always written solid. However, there are a few important exceptions.

downtown
upstairs
onstage
offhand
   but
in-house
off-line
on-line

42. Compound adverbs of more than two words are usually written open, and they usually follow the words they modify.

every which way	hook, line, and sinker
little by little	off and on
high and dry	over and over

43. A few three-word adverbs are spelled like hyphenated adjectives and are therefore written with hyphens. But many adverbs are written open even if the adjective is hyphenated.

back-to-back (adverb or adjective)
face-to-face (adverb or adjective)
   but
hand-to-hand combat
fought hand to hand
off-the-cuff remarks
spoke off the cuff

Compound Verbs

44. Two-word verbs consisting of a verb followed by an adverb or a preposition are written open.

get together	strike out
break through	run across
run around	put down
run wild	print out

45. A compound composed of a particle followed by a verb is written solid.

upgrade	overcome
outflank	bypass

46. A verb derived from an open or hyphenated compound noun is hyphenated.

blue-pencil	tap-dance
sweet-talk	poor-mouth
double-check	water-ski

47. A verb derived from a solid noun is written solid.

bankroll
roughhouse
mainstream

Compounds Formed with Word Elements

Many new and temporary compounds are formed by adding word elements to existing words or by combining word elements. There are three basic word elements: prefixes (such as *anti-, re-, non-, super-*), suffixes (such as *-er, -ly, -ness, -ism*), and combining forms (such as *mini-, macro-, pseud-, ortho-, -ped, -graphy, -gamic, -plasty*). Prefixes and suffixes are usually attached to existing words; combining forms are usually combined to form new words.

48. prefix + word Except as specified in the paragraphs below, compounds formed from a prefix and a word are usually written solid.

precondition	suborder
interagency	overfond
refurnish	postwar
misshapen	unhelpful

49. If the prefix ends with a vowel and the word it is attached to begins with the same vowel, the compound is usually hyphenated.

> anti-inflation
> co-owner
> de-emphasize

However, there are many exceptions.

> cooperate
> reentry
> preempt

50. If the base word to which a prefix is added is capitalized, the compound is hyphenated.

> anti-American   pre-Columbian
> post-Victorian   inter-Caribbean

The prefix is usually not capitalized in such compounds. But if the prefix and the base word together form a new proper name, the compound may be solid with the prefix capitalized.

> Postimpressionist
> Precambrian

51. Compounds made with *self-* and *ex-* meaning "former" are hyphenated.

> self-pity
> ex-wife

52. If a prefix is added to a hyphenated compound, it may be either followed by a hyphen or closed up solid to the next element. Permanent compounds of this kind should be checked in a dictionary.

unair-conditioned	non-self-governing
ultra-up-to-date	unself-conscious

53. In typewritten and keyboarded material, if a prefix is added to an open compound, the prefix is followed by a hyphen. In typeset material, this hyphen is often represented by an en dash. (For more on this use of the en dash, see paragraph 13 on page 39.)

> ex–Boy Scout
> post–coup d'état

54. A compound that would be identical with another word if written solid is usually hyphenated to prevent misreading.

> a multi-ply fabric
> re-collect the money
> un-ionized particles

55. A compound that might otherwise be solid may be hyphenated if it could be momentarily puzzling.

> coed *or* co-ed
> coworker *or* co-worker
> overreact *or* over-react
> interrow *or* inter-row

56. Temporary compounds formed from *vice-* are usually hyphenated; however, some permanent compounds (such as *vice president* and *vice admiral*) are open.

57. When prefixes are attached to numerals, the compounds are hyphenated.

> pre-1982 expenses
> post-1975 vintages
> non-20th-century ideas

58. Compounds created from combining forms like *Anglo-*, *Judeo-*, or *Sino-* are hyphenated when the second element is an independent word. They are written solid when it is a combining form.

> Judeo-Christian   Anglophobe
> Austro-Hungarian   Francophone
> Sino-Soviet   Italophile

59. Prefixes that are repeated in the same compound are separated by a hyphen.

> sub-subheading

60. Some prefixes and initial combining forms have related independent adjectives or adverbs that may be used where the prefix might be expected. A temporary compound with *quasi(-)* or *pseudo(-)* therefore may be written open as modifier + noun, or hyphenated as combining form + noun.

> quasi intellectual *or* quasi-intellectual
> pseudo liberal *or* pseudo-liberal

In some cases (such as *super, super-*), the independent modifier may not have quite the same meaning as the prefix.

61. Compounds consisting of different prefixes with the same base word and joined by *and* or *or* are shortened by pruning the first compound back to a hyphenated prefix, followed by a space.

> pre- and postoperative care
> anti- or pro-Revolutionary sympathies.

62. word + suffix Except as noted in the paragraphs below, compounds formed by adding a suffix to a word are written solid.

> Darwinist landscaper
> fortyish powerlessness

63. Permanent or temporary compounds formed with a suffix are hyphenated if the addition of the suffix would create a sequence of three identical letters.

> bell-like
> will-less
> a coffee-er coffee

64. Temporary compounds made with a suffix are often hyphenated if the base word is more than two syllables long, if the base word ends with the same letter the suffix begins with, or if the suffix creates a confusing sequence of letters.

> industry-wide tunnel-like
> umbrella-like jaw-wards
> American-ness battle-worthy

65. Compounds made from a number + *odd* are hyphenated whether the number is spelled out or in numerals; a number + *-fold* is solid if the number is spelled out but hyphenated if it is in numerals.

20-odd	twenty-odd
12-fold	twelvefold

66. Most compounds formed from an open or hyphenated compound + a suffix do not separate the suffix by a hyphen. But such suffixes as *-like*, *-wide*, *-worthy*, and *-proof*, all of which exist as independent adjectives, are attached by a hyphen.

good-humoredness
dollar-a-yearism
do-it-yourselfer
a United Nations-like agency

Open compounds often become hyphenated when a suffix is added unless they are proper nouns.

middle age   *but*   middle-ager
tough guy   *but*   tough-guyese
New Englandism
Wall Streeter

67. combining form + combining form   Many new terms in technical fields are created by adding combining form to combining form or combining form to a word or word part. Such compounds are generally intended to be permanent, even though many never get into the dictionary. They are normally written solid.

    macrographic
    pseudoserial

Miscellaneous Styling Conventions

68. Compounds that would otherwise be written solid according to the principles described above may be written open or hyphenated to avoid ambiguity, to ensure rapid comprehension, or to make the pronunciation clearer.

re-utter	tri-city
bi-level	un-iced
umbrella-like	meat-ax *or* meat ax

69. When typographical features such as capitals or italics make word relationships in a sentence clear, it is not necessary to hyphenate an open compound.

    his America First sign
    a *Chicago Tribune* story
    an "eyes only" memo

70. Publications (such as technical journals) aimed at a specialized readership likely to recognize the elements of a compound tend to use open and solid stylings more frequently than general publications do.

    electrooculogram
    radiofrequency
    rapid eye movement

71. Words that are formed by reduplication and so consist of two similar-sounding elements (such as *hush-hush*, *razzle-dazzle*, or *hugger-mugger*) present styling questions like those of compounds. Words like these are hyphenated if each of the elements is made up of more than one syllable. If each element has only one syllable, the words are often written solid. However, for very short words (such as *no-no*, *go-go*, and *so-so*), words in which both elements may have primary stress (such as *tip-top* and *sci-fi*), and words coined in the twentieth century (such as *ack-ack* and *hush-hush*), the hyphenated styling is more common.

goody-goody	peewee
teeter-totter	knickknack
topsy-turvy	singsong
crisscross	boo-boo

Chapter 4

Abbreviations

Abbreviations are used for a variety of reasons: to save space, to avoid repetition of long words and phrases, to save time, or simply to conform to conventional usage.

Unfortunately, the contemporary styling of abbreviations is inconsistent and arbitrary. No set of rules can hope to cover all the possible variations, exceptions, and peculiarities encountered in print. The styling of abbreviations—capitalized vs. lowercased, closed-up vs. spaced, punctuated vs. unpunctuated—depends most often on a writer's preference or an organization's policy.

All is not complete confusion, however. Some abbreviations (such as *e.g., etc., i.e., No.,* and *viz.*) are almost always punctuated, while others that are pronounced as words (such as *NATO, NASA, NOW, OPEC,* and *SALT*) tend to be all-capitalized and unpunctuated. Punctuated abbreviations are always closed up except when each abbreviated word has two or more letters (as in *lt. gov.* and *rec. sec.*). Styling problems can be dealt with by consulting a good general dictionary such as *Merriam-Webster's Collegiate Dictionary, Tenth Edition,* especially for capitalization guidance, and by following the guidelines of one's own organization. An abbreviations dictionary such as *Webster's Guide to Abbreviations* may also be helpful.

Punctuation

The paragraphs that follow provide a few broad principles that apply to abbreviations in general. However, there are many specific situations in which these principles will not apply. The section on Specific Styling Conventions, beginning on page 159, contains information on these situations and on particular kinds of abbreviations.

1. A period follows most abbreviations that are formed by omitting all but the first few letters of a word.

   bull. [for *bulletin*]
   bro. [for *brother*]
   fig. [for *figure*]
   Fr. [for *French*]

2. A period follows most abbreviations that are formed by omitting letters from the middle of a word.

   secy. [for *secretary*]
   mfg. [for *manufacturing*]

agcy. [for *agency*]
Mr. [for *Mister*]

3. Punctuation is usually omitted from abbreviations that are made up of initial letters of words that constitute a phrase or compound word. However, for some of these abbreviations, especially ones that are not capitalized, the punctuation is retained.

GNP [for *gross national product*]
EFT [for *electronic funds transfer*]
PC [for *personal computer*]
f.o.b. [for *free on board*]

4. Terms in which a suffix is added to a numeral, such as *1st, 2nd, 3d, 8vo,* and *12mo,* are not abbreviations and do not require a period.

5. Isolated letters of the alphabet used to designate a shape or position in a sequence are not abbreviations and are not punctuated.

T square   I beam
A 1   V sign

6. Some abbreviations are punctuated with one or more slashes in place of periods.

c/o [for *care of*]
d/b/a [for *doing business as*]
w/o [for *without*]
w/w [for *wall to wall*]

Capitalization

1. Abbreviations are capitalized if the words they represent are proper nouns or adjectives.

    F [for *Fahrenheit*]
    NBC [for *National Broadcasting Company*]
    Nov. [for *November*]
    Brit. [for *British*]

2. Abbreviations are usually all-capitalized when they represent single letters of words that are normally lowercased. There are, however, some very common abbreviations formed in this way that are not capitalized.

    TM [for *trademark*]
    ETA [for *estimated time of arrival*]
    CATV [for *community antenna television*]
    EEG [for *electroencephalogram*]
    FY [for *fiscal year*]
    a.k.a. [for *also known as*]
    d/b/a [for *doing business as*]

3. Most acronyms that are pronounced as words, rather than as a series of letters, are capitalized. If they have been assimilated into the language as words in their own right, however, they are most often lowercased.

OPEC	quasar
NATO	laser
MIRV	sonar
NOW account	scuba

Plurals, Possessives, and Compounds

1. Punctuated abbreviations of single words are pluralized by adding *-s* before the period.

bldgs.	figs.
bros.	mts.

2. Punctuated abbreviations that stand for phrases or compounds are pluralized by adding *-'s* after the last period.

Ph.D.'s	J.P.'s
f.o.b.'s	M.B.A.'s

3. Unpunctuated abbreviations that stand for phrases or compound words are usually pluralized by adding *-s* to the end of the abbreviation.

COLAs	PCs
CPUs	DOSs

4. The plural form of most lowercase single-letter abbreviations is made by repeating the letter. For the plural form of single-letter abbreviations that are abbreviations for units of measure, see paragraph 5 below.

cc. [for *copies*]
ll. [for *lines*]
pp. [for *pages*]
nn. [for *notes*]
vv. [for *verses*]
ff. [for *and the following ones*]

5. The plural form of abbreviations of units of measure is the same as the singular form. (For details on punctuation, see paragraph 48 on page 173.)

30 sec.	20 min.
30 d.	50 m
24 ml	200 bbl.
24 h.	10 mi.

6. Possessives of abbreviations are formed in the same way as those of spelled-out nouns: the singular possessive is formed by adding *-'s*, the plural possessive simply by adding an apostrophe.

the CPU's memory
Brody Corp.'s earnings
most CPUs' memories
Bay Bros.' annual sale

7. Compounds that consist of an abbreviation added to another word are formed in the same way as compounds that consist of spelled-out nouns.

a Kalamazoo, Mich.-based company
an AMA-approved medical school

8. Compounds formed by adding a prefix or suffix to an abbreviation are usually written with a hyphen.

an IBM-like organization
non-DNA molecules
pre-HEW years

Specific Styling Conventions

The following paragraphs, arranged alphabetically, describe practices commonly followed for specific kinds of situations involving abbreviations.

A and An

1. The choice of the article *a* or *an* before abbreviations depends on the sound with which the abbreviation begins. If an abbreviation begins with a consonant sound, *a* is normally used; if an abbreviation begins with a vowel sound, *an* is used. (For more on the use of *a* and *an*, see paragraphs 3–5 on pages 231–32.)

    a B.A. degree   an FCC report
    a YMCA club   an SAT score
    a UN agency   an IRS agent

A.D. and B.C.

2. The abbreviations A.D. and B.C. usually appear in typeset matter as punctuated, unspaced small capitals; in typed material they usually appear as punctuated, unspaced capitals.

3. The abbreviation A.D. usually precedes the date; the abbreviation B.C. follows the date. However, many writers place A.D. after the date as well. In references to whole centuries,

A.D. follows the century. (For more details, see paragraph 14 on pages 192–93.)

A.D. 185   *but also*   185 A.D.
41 B.C.
the fourth century A.D.

Agencies and Organizations

4. The names of agencies, associations, and organizations are usually abbreviated after they have been spelled out on their first occurrence in a text. The abbreviations are usually all-capitalized and unpunctuated.

EPA	NCAA
SEC	USO
NAACP	NOW

In contexts where the abbreviation will be recognized, it may be used without having its full form spelled out on its first occurrence.

Beginning a Sentence

5. Most writers avoid beginning a sentence with an abbreviation that is ordinarily not capitalized. Abbreviations that are ordinarily capitalized, on the other hand, are commonly used to begin sentences.

Page 22 contains . . .   *not*   P. 22 contains . . .
Doctor Smith believes . . .   *or*   Dr. Smith believes . . .
OSHA regulations require . . .

Books of the Bible

6. Books of the Bible are generally spelled out in running text but abbreviated in references to chapter and verse.

> The minister based the sermon on Genesis.
>
> In the beginning God created the heavens and the earth.—Gen. 1:1

Company Names

7. The styling of company names varies widely. Many writers avoid abbreviating any part of a company's name unless the abbreviation is part of the official name. However, others routinely abbreviate words such as *Company, Corporation,* and *Incorporated.* Words such as *Airlines, Associates, Fabricators,* and *Manufacturing,* however, are spelled out.

> McGraw-Hill Book Company
> *or* McGraw-Hill Book Co.

An ampersand (&) frequently replaces the word *and* in official company names. For more on this use of the ampersand, see paragraph 1 on pages 2–3.

8. If a company is easily recognizable from its initials, its name is usually spelled out for the first mention and abbreviated in all subsequent references. Some companies have made their initials part of their official name, and in those cases the initials appear in all references.

General Motors Corp. released its first-quarter earnings figures today. A GM spokesperson said . . .

MCM Electronics, an Ohio-based company . . .

Compass Points

9. Compass points are abbreviated when occurring after street names; these abbreviations may be punctuated and may be preceded by a comma. When a compass point precedes the word *Street, Avenue,* etc., it is usually spelled out in full.

> 2122 Fourteenth Street, NW
> *or* 2122 Fourteenth Street NW
> *or* 2122 Fourteenth Street, N.W.
> 192 East 49th Street
> 1282 North Avenue

Contractions

10. Some abbreviations resemble contractions by including an apostrophe in place of omitted letters. These abbreviations are not punctuated with a period. (This style of abbreviation is usually avoided in formal correspondence.)

> sec'y [for *secretary*]
> ass'n [for *association*]
> dep't [for *department*]

Dates

11. The names of days and months should not be abbreviated in running text. The names of months usually are not abbreviated in date-

lines of business letters, but they may be abbreviated in government or military correspondence.

the December issue of *Scientific American*
a meeting held on August 1, 1985
   not   a meeting held on Aug. 1, 1985
business dateline: November 1, 1985
military dateline: 1 Nov 85

Degrees

12. Except for a few academic degrees with highly recognizable abbreviations (such as *A.B., M.S.,* and *Ph.D.*), the names of degrees and professional ratings are spelled out in full when first mentioned. Often the name of the degree is followed by its abbreviation enclosed in parentheses, so that the abbreviation may be used alone later. When a degree or professional rating follows a person's name, it is usually abbreviated.

Special attention is devoted to the master of arts in teaching (M.A.T.) degree.
Julia Ramirez, J.D.

13. Like other abbreviations, abbreviations of degrees and professional ratings are often unpunctuated. In general, punctuated abbreviations are more common for academic degrees, and unpunctuated abbreviations are slightly more common for professional ratings, especially if the latter consist of three or more capitalized letters.

Ph.D.	R.Ph.
B.Sc.	CLU
M.B.A.	RDMS

14. The first letter of each element in abbreviations of all degrees and professional ratings is capitalized. Letters other than the first letter are usually not capitalized.

D.Ch.E.	M.F.A.
Litt.D.	D.Th.

Division of Abbreviations

15. Division of abbreviations at the end of lines or between pages should be avoided.

Full Forms

16. When using an abbreviation that may be unfamiliar or confusing to the reader, many writers give the full form first, followed by the abbreviation in parentheses. In subsequent references, just the abbreviation is used.

first reference: At the American Bar Association (ABA) meeting in June . . .

subsequent reference: At that particular ABA meeting . . .

Geographical Names

17. U.S. Postal Service abbreviations for states, possessions, and Canadian provinces are all-capitalized and unpunctuated, as are Postal Service abbreviations for streets and other geographical features when these abbreviations are used on envelopes addressed for automated mass handling.

regular address style:	1234 Cross Blvd.
	Sayville, MN 56789
automated handling:	1234 CROSS BLVD
	SAYVILLE, MN 56789

18. Abbreviations of states are often used in running text to identify the location of a city or county. In this context the traditional state abbreviations are usually used, set off with commas. In other situations within running text, the names of states are usually not abbreviated.

John Slade of 15 Chestnut St., Sarasota, Fla., has won . . .

the Louisville, Ky., public library system

Boston, the largest city in Massachusetts, . . .

19. Terms such as *street, road,* and *boulevard* may be either abbreviated or unabbreviated in running text. When they are abbreviated, they are punctuated.

an accident on Windward Road [*or* Rd.]

our office at 1234 Cross Blvd. [*or* Boulevard]

20. Names of countries are usually spelled in full in running text. The most common exception is the abbreviation *U.S.* (see paragraph 22 below).

Great Britain and the U.S. announced the agreement.

21. Abbreviations for the names of most countries are punctuated. Abbreviations for countries whose names include more than one word are often not punctuated if the abbreviations are formed from only the initial letters of the individual words.

Mex.	Gt. Brit.
Can.	U.K. *or* UK
Ger.	U.S. *or* US

22. *United States* is often abbreviated when used as an adjective. When used as a noun, it is usually spelled out, or it is spelled on its initial use and then abbreviated in subsequent references.

U.S. Department of Justice
U.S. foreign policy
The United States has offered to . . .

23. *Saint* is usually abbreviated when it is part of the name of a geographical or topographical feature. *Mount, Point,* and *Fort* may be either spelled out or abbreviated, according to individual preference. *Saint, Mount,* and *Point* are normally abbreviated when space is at a premium. (For more on the abbreviation of *Saint,* see paragraph 35 below.)

St. Louis, Missouri	Mount McKinley
St. Kitts	Point Pelee
Mount St. Helens	Fort Sumter

Latin Words and Phrases

24. Words and phrases derived from Latin are commonly abbreviated in contexts where readers can be expected to recognize them. They are punctuated, lowercased, and usually not italicized.

etc.	viz.
i.e.	et al.
e.g.	ibid.

Latitude and Longitude

25. Latitude and longitude are abbreviated in tabular data but written out in running text.

in a table: lat. 10°20′N *or* lat. 10-20N

in text: from 10°20′ north latitude to 10°30′ south latitude

Laws and Bylaws

26. Laws and bylaws are spelled in full when first mentioned; in subsequent references they may be abbreviated.

first reference: Article I, Section 1

subsequent reference: Art. I, Sec. 1

Military Ranks and Units

27. Military ranks are usually given in full when used with a surname only, but are abbreviated when used with a full name.

Colonel Howe
Col. John P. Howe

28. In nonmilitary correspondence, abbreviations for military ranks are often punctuated and set in capital and lowercase letters.

in the military: BG John T. Dow, USA
                      LCDR Mary I. Lee, USN
                      Col S. J. Smith, USMC

outside the military: Brig. Gen. John T. Dow, USA
                      Lt. Comdr. Mary I. Lee, USN
                      Col. S. J. Smith, USMC

29. Abbreviations for military units are capitalized and unpunctuated.

USA   SAC
USAF   NORAD

Number

30. The word *number,* when used with figures such as *1* or *2* to indicate a rank or rating, is usually abbreviated to *No.*

The No. 1 priority is to promote profitability.

31. The word *number* is usually abbreviated when it is part of a set unit (such as a contract number).

Contract No. N-1234-76-57
Policy No. 123-5-X
Publ. Nos. 12 and 13
Index No. 7855

Personal Names

32. First names are not usually abbreviated.

> George S. Patterson   *not*   Geo. S. Patterson

33. Unspaced initials of famous persons are sometimes used in place of their full names. The initials may or may not be punctuated.

> FDR   *or*   F.D.R.

34. When initials are used with a surname, they are spaced and punctuated.

> F. D. Roosevelt

Saint

35. The word *Saint* is often abbreviated when used before the name of a saint or when it is the first element of the name of a city or institution named after a saint. However, when it forms part of a surname, it may or may not be abbreviated. Surnames and names of institutions should follow the style used by the person or the institution.

> St. Peter   *or*   Saint Peter
> St. Cloud, Minnesota
> St. John's University
> Augustus Saint-Gaudens
> Louis St. Laurent
> Saint Joseph College

Scientific Terms

36. In binomial nomenclature, a genus name may be abbreviated with its initial letter after the first reference to it is spelled out. The abbreviation is always punctuated.

first reference: *Escherichia coli*
subsequent reference: *E. coli*

37. Abbreviations for the names of chemical compounds or mechanical or electronic equipment or processes are usually not punctuated.

    PCB   CPU
    OCR   PBX

38. The symbols for chemical elements are not punctuated.

    H   Pb
    Cl   Na

Time

39. When time is expressed in figures, the abbreviations that follow are most often written as punctuated lowercase letters; punctuated small capital letters are also common. (For more on the use of *a.m.* and *p.m.*, see paragraph 43 on pages 203–4.)

    8:30 a.m.   *or*   8:30 A.M.
    10:00 p.m.   *or*   10:00 P.M.

40. In transportation schedules, *a.m.* and *p.m.* are generally written in capitalized, unpunctuated, unspaced letters.

    8:30 AM
    10:00 PM

41. Time-zone designations are usually written in capitalized, unpunctuated, unspaced letters.

    EST

    PST

    CDT

Titles

42. The only courtesy titles that are always abbreviated in written references are *Mr., Ms., Mrs.,* and *Messrs.* Other titles, such as *Doctor, Representative,* or *Senator,* may be either written out or abbreviated.

    Ms. Lee A. Downs

    Messrs. Lake, Mason, and Nambeth

    Doctor Howe   *or*   Dr. Howe

43. Despite some traditional objections, the titles *Honorable* and *Reverend* are often abbreviated, with and without *the* preceding the titles.

    the Honorable Samuel I. O'Leary

      or [the] Hon. Samuel I. O'Leary

    the Reverend Samuel I. O'Leary

      or [the] Rev. Samuel I. O'Leary

44. The designations *Jr.* and *Sr.* may be used with courtesy titles, with abbreviations for academic degrees, and with professional-rating abbreviations. They may or may not be preceded by a comma, according to the writer's preference. They are only used with a full name.

Mr. John K. Walker, Jr.
General John K. Walker Jr.
The Honorable John K. Walker, Jr.
John K. Walker Jr., M.D.

45. When an abbreviation for an academic degree, professional certification, or association membership follows a name, it is usually preceded by a comma. No courtesy title should precede the name.

Dr. Jesse Smith   *or*   Jesse Smith, M.D.
    but not   Dr. Jesse Smith, M.D.
Katherine Derwinski, CLU
Carol Manning, M.D., FACPS

46. The abbreviation *Esq.* for *Esquire* is used in the United States after the surname of professional persons such as attorneys, architects, consuls, clerks of the court, and justices of the peace. It is not used, however, if a courtesy title such as *Dr., Hon., Miss, Mr., Mrs.,* or *Ms.* precedes the first name.

Carolyn B. West, Esq.

Units of Measure

47. Measures and weights may be abbreviated in figure-plus-unit combinations. However, if the numeral is written out, the unit should also be written out.

15 cu ft   *or*   15 cu. ft.   *but*   fifteen cubic feet
How many cubic feet does the refrigerator hold?

48. Abbreviations for metric units are usually not punctuated. Abbreviations for traditional units are usually punctuated.

14 ml	8 ft.
12 km	4 sec.
22 mi.	20 min.

Versus

49. *Versus* is usually abbreviated as "v." in legal contexts; it is either spelled out or abbreviated as lowercase roman letters "vs." in general contexts. For more on the use of *v.* in legal contexts, see paragraph 35 on page 91.

in a legal context: Smith v. *Vermont*
in a general context: honesty versus dishonesty
                                           or
                                    honesty vs. dishonesty

Chapter 5

Numbers

The styling of numbers presents special difficulties to writers because there are so many conventions to follow, some of which may conflict when applied to particular passages. Your major decision will be whether to write out numbers or to express them in figures, and usage varies considerably on this point.

Numbers as Words or Figures

At one extreme of styling, all numbers, sometimes even including dates, are written out. This usage is uncommon and is usually limited to proclamations, legal documents, and some other types of very formal writing. At the other extreme, some types of technical writing, such as statistical reports, contain no written-out numbers except sometimes at the beginning of a sentence.

In general, figures are easier to read than spelled-out numbers; however, the spelled-out forms are helpful in certain circumstances, such as in distinguishing different categories of numbers or in providing relief from an overwhelming cluster of numerals. Most writers follow one or the other of two common conventions combining numerals and written-out numbers. The conventions are described in this section, along with the exceptions to the general rules.

Basic Conventions

1. The first system requires that a writer use words for numbers up through nine and figures for exact numbers greater than nine. (A variation of this system sets the number ten as the dividing point.) In this system, numbers that consist of a whole number between one and nine followed by *hundred, thousand, million,* etc., may either be spelled out or expressed in figures.

> She performed in 22 plays on Broadway, seven of which won awards.
>
> The new edition will consist of 25 volumes, which will be issued at a rate of approximately four volumes per year.
>
> The cat show attracted an unexpected two thousand entries.
>
> They sold more than 2,000 units in the first year.

2. The second system requires that a writer use figures for all exact numbers 100 and

above (or 101 and above) and words for numbers from one through ninety-nine (or one through one hundred) and for numbers that consist of a whole number between one and ninety-nine followed by *hundred, thousand, million,* etc.

> The artist spent nearly twelve years completing these four volumes, which comprise 435 hand-colored engravings.

> The 145 seminar participants toured the area's eighteen period houses.

> In the course of four hours, the popular author signed twenty-five hundred copies of her new book.

Sentence Beginnings

3. Numbers that begin a sentence are written out, although some writers make an exception for dates. Avoid spelled-out numbers that are lengthy and awkward by restructuring the sentence so that the number appears elsewhere than at the beginning and may then be written as a figure.

> Sixty-two new models will be introduced this year.
>
> *or*
>
> There will be 62 new models introduced this year.
>
> Nineteen eighty-seven was our best earnings year so far.
>
> *or*
>
> 1987 was our best earnings year so far.
>
> One hundred fifty-seven illustrations, including 86 color plates, are contained in the book.

or

The book contains 157 illustrations, including 86 color plates.

Adjacent or Paired Numbers

4. Generally, two separate sets of figures should not be written adjacent to one another in running text unless they form a series. In order to avoid the juxtaposition of unrelated figures, either the sentence should be rephrased or one of the figures should be spelled out—usually the figure with the written form that is shorter and more easily read.

> sixteen ½-inch dowels
> twenty-five 11-inch platters
> twenty 100-point games
> 78 twenty-point games
> By 1997, thirty schools . . .

5. Numbers paired at the beginning of a sentence are usually written alike. If the first word of the sentence is a spelled-out number, the second, related number is also spelled out. However, some writers prefer that each number be styled independently, even if that results in an inconsistent pairing.

> Sixty to seventy-five copies will be required.
> Sixty to 75 copies will be required.

6. Numbers that form a pair or a series referring to comparable quantities within a sentence or a paragraph should be treated consistently. The style of the largest number

usually determines the style of the other numbers. Thus, a series of numbers including some that would ordinarily be spelled out might all be written as figures. Similarly, figures are used to express all the numbers in a series if one of those numbers is a mixed or simple fraction.

> The three jobs took 5, 12, and 4½ hours, respectively.
>
> We need four desks, three chairs, fourteen file cabinets, and six computers.

Round Numbers

7. Approximate or round numbers, particularly those that can be expressed in one or two words, are often written out in general writing; in technical and scientific writing they are more likely to be expressed as numerals.

> seven hundred people
> five thousand years
> four hundred thousand volumes
> *but in technical writing*
> 50,000 people per year
> 20,000 species of fish

8. For easier reading, numbers of one million and above may be expressed as figures followed by the word *million, billion,* and so forth. The figure may include a decimal fraction, but the fraction is not usually carried past the first digit to the right of the decimal

point, and it is never carried past the third digit. If a more exact number is required, the whole amount should be written in figures.

about 4.6 billion years old
1.2 million metric tons of grain
the last 600 million years
   but 200,000 years *not* 200 thousand years
$7.25 million
$3,456,000,000

Ordinal Numbers

1. Ordinal numbers generally follow the styling rules for cardinal numbers. In technical writing, however, ordinal numbers are usually written as figure-plus-suffix combinations. In addition, certain ordinal numbers—for example, those specifying percentiles and latitudinal lines—are usually set as figures.

the sixth Robert de Bruce
the ninth grade
the 9th and 14th chapters
the 98th Congress
the 7th percentile
the 40th parallel

2. The forms *second* and *third* may be written with figures as *2d* or *2nd, 3d* or *3rd, 22d* or *22nd, 93d* or *93rd, 102d* or *102nd,* etc. A period does not follow the suffix.

Roman Numerals

Roman numerals are generally used in the specific situations described below.

1. Roman numerals are traditionally used to differentiate rulers and popes with identical names.

   Elizabeth II   Innocent X
   Henry VIII   Louis XIV

2. Roman numerals are used to differentiate related males who have the same name. The numerals are used only with a person's full name and are placed after the surname with no intervening comma. Ordinals are sometimes used instead of Roman numerals.

   James R. Watson II
   James R. Watson 2nd *or* 2d

   Possessives for these names are formed as follows:

   singular: James R. Watson III's [*or* 3rd's *or* 3d's] house

   plural: the James R. Watson IIIs' [*or* 3rds' *or* 3ds'] house

3. Lowercase Roman numerals (i, ii, iii, iv, etc.) are often used to number the pages of a publication that precede the regular Arabic sequence, as in a foreword, preface, or introduction.

4. Roman numerals are often used in outlines and in lists of major headings. For an example of an outline, see paragraph 20 on page 196.

5. Roman numerals are found as part of a few established technical terms such as blood-clotting factors, quadrant numbers, designations of cranial nerves, and virus or organism types. Also, chords in the study of music harmony are designated by capital and lowercase Roman numerals (often followed by small Arabic numbers). For the most part, however, technical terms that include numbers express them in Arabic form.

> blood-clotting factor VII
> quadrant III
> the cranial nerves II and IX
> Population II stars
> type I error
> vii$_6$ chord
> HIV-III virus
> *but*
> adenosine 3′,5′-monophosphate
> cesium 137
> PL/1 programming language

Punctuation and Plurals

The paragraphs that follow provide general rules for the use of commas and hyphens in compound and large numbers, as well as the plural forms of numbers. For specific categories of numbers, such as dates, money, and decimal fractions, see the section on Specific Styling Conventions beginning on page 187.

Commas in Large Numbers

1. In general writing, with the exceptions explained in paragraph 3 below, figures of four digits may be written with or without a comma; the punctuated form is more common. If the numerals form part of a tabulation, commas are necessary so that four-digit numerals can align with numerals of five or more digits.

> 2,000 case histories
> *or less commonly*   1253 people

2. Whole numbers of five digits or more (but not decimal fractions) use a comma to separate three-digit groups, counting from the right.

> a fee of $12,500
> 15,000 units
> a population of 1,500,000

3. Certain types of numbers are treated differently. Decimal fractions and serial and multi-digit numbers in set combinations, such as the numbers of policies, contracts, checks, streets, rooms, suites, telephones, pages, military hours, and years, do not contain commas.

2.5544   Room 1206
Policy No. 33442   1650 hours
check 34567   the year 1929

Hyphens

4. Hyphens are used with written-out numbers between 21 and 99.

> forty-one
> forty-first
> four hundred twenty-two

5. A hyphen is used between the numerator and the denominator of a fraction that is written out when that fraction is used as a modifier. A written-out fraction consisting of two words only (such as *two thirds*) is usually left open, although the hyphenated form is also common. Multiword numerators and denominators are usually hyphenated. If either the numerator or the denominator is hyphenated, no hyphen is used between them. (For more on fractions, see the section beginning on page 197.)

> a two-thirds vote
> three fifths of her paycheck
> seven and four fifths
> forty-five hundredths
> four five-hundredths

6. Numbers that form the first part of a compound modifier expressing measurement are followed by a hyphen, except when the second part of the modifier is the word *percent*.

a 5-foot board
a 28-mile trip
a 10-pound weight
an eight-pound baby
a 680-acre ranch
a 75 percent reduction

7. An adjective or adverb made from a numeral plus the suffix *-fold* contains a hyphen, while a similar term made from a written-out number is closed up. (For more on the use of suffixes with numbers, see paragraphs 62 and 65 on pages 149 and 150 respectively.)

increased 20-fold
a fourfold increase

8. Serial numbers, such as Social Security or engine numbers, often contain hyphens that make lengthy numerals more readable.

020-42-1691

9. Numbers should not be divided at the end of a line. If division is unavoidable, the break occurs only after a comma. End-of-line breaks do not occur at decimal points, and a name with a numerical suffix (such as Robert F. Walker III) is not divided between the name and the numeral.

Inclusive Numbers

10. Inclusive numbers—those which express a range—are separated either by the word *to*

or by a hyphen or en dash, which means "(up) to and including" when used between dates and other inclusive numbers. (For more on the en dash, see paragraph 13 on page 39.)

> pages 40 to 98
> pages 40–98
> pp. 40–98
> the fiscal year 1987–88
> spanning the years 1915 to 1941
> the decade 1920–1930

Inclusive numbers separated by a hyphen or en dash are not used in combination with the words *from* or *between,* as in "from 1955–60" or "between 1970–90." Instead, phrases like these are written as "from 1955 to 1960" or "between 1970 and 1990."

11. Units of measurement expressed in words or abbreviations are usually used only after the second element of an inclusive number. Symbols, however, are repeated.

> an increase in dosage from 200 to 500 mg
> ten to fifteen dollars
> 30 to 35 degrees Celsius
> *but*
> $50 to $60 million
> 45° to 48° F

12. Numbers that are part of an inclusive set or range are usually styled alike: figures with figures, spelled-out words with other spelled-

out words. Similarly, approximate numbers
are usually not paired with exact numbers.

> from 8 to 108 absences
> five to twenty guests
> 300,000,000 to 305,000,000
>   *not*   300 million to 305,000,000

13. Inclusive page numbers and dates may be
written in full or elided (i.e., shortened).
However, inclusive dates that appear in titles
and other headings are almost never elided.
Dates that appear with era designations are
also not elided (see also paragraph 14 on
pages 192–93).

> 467–68   *or*   467–468
> 203–4   *or*   203–204
> 1724–27   *or*   1724–1727
> 1463–1510
> 1800–1801
> 552–549 B.C.

Elided numbers are used because they save
space. The most commonly used style for the
elision of inclusive numbers is based on the
following rules:

a. Never elide inclusive numbers that have
only two digits: 33–37, *not* 33–7.

b. Never elide inclusive numbers when the
first number ends in 00: 100–108, *not*
100–08 *and not* 100–8.

c. In other numbers, do not omit the tens
digit from the higher number: 232–34.

Exception: Where the tens digit of both numbers is zero, write only one digit for the higher number: 103–4, *not* 103–04.

Plurals

14. The plurals of written-out numbers are formed by adding *-s* or *-es*.

> Back in the thirties these roads were unpaved.
> Christmas shoppers bought the popular toy in twos and threes.

15. The plurals of figures are formed by adding *-s*. Some writers prefer to add an apostrophe before the *-s*. (For more on the plurals of figures, see paragraphs 18–19 on page 120 and paragraph 5 on pages 4–5.)

> This ghost town was booming back in the 1840s.
> The first two artificial hearts to be implanted in human patients were Jarvik-7s.
> *but also*
> 1's and 7's that looked alike

Specific Styling Conventions

The following paragraphs, arranged alphabetically, describe styling practices commonly followed for specific situations involving numbers.

Addresses

1. Arabic numerals are used for all building, house, apartment, room, and suite numbers except for *one*, which is written out.

6 Lincoln Road
1436 Fremont Street
   but
One Bayside Drive

When the address of a building is used as its name, the number in the address is often written out.

Fifty Maple Street

2. Numbered streets have their numbers written as ordinals. There are two distinct styling conventions. Under the first, numbered street names from First through Twelfth are written out, and numerals are used for all numbered streets above Twelfth. Under the second, all numbered street names up to and including One Hundredth are spelled out.

167 Second Avenue
19 South 22nd Street
122 East Forty-second Street
145 East 145th Street
in the Sixties [streets from 60th to 69th]
in the 120s [streets from 120th to 129th]

When a house or building number immediately precedes a street number, a spaced hyphen may be inserted between the two numbers, or the street number may be written out.

2018 - 14th Street
2018 Fourteenth Street

3. Arabic numerals are used to designate highways and, in some states, county roads.

Interstate 91   *or*   I-91
U.S. Route 1   *or*   U.S. 1
Massachusetts 57
County 213

Dates

4. Year numbers are written as figures. If a number representing a year begins a sentence, it may be spelled out or the sentence may be rewritten to avoid beginning it with a figure. (For additional examples, see paragraph 3 on pages 176–77.)

1995
1888–96
Fifteen eighty-eight marked the end to Spanish ambitions for the control of England.
or
Spanish ambitions for the control of England ended in 1588.

5. A year number may be abbreviated, or cut back to its last two digits, in informal writing or when an event is so well known that it needs no century designation. In these cases an apostrophe precedes the numerals. (For more on this use of the apostrophe, see paragraph 5 on pages 4–5.)

He always maintained that he'd graduated from Korea, Clash of '52.
the blizzard of '88

6. Full dates (month, day, and year) may be written in one of two ways. The traditional style is the month-day-year sequence, with the year set off by commas that precede and follow it. An alternative style is the inverted date, or day-month-year sequence, which does not require commas. This sequence is used in U.S. government publications and in the military.

traditional: July 8, 1776, was a warm, sunny day in Philadelphia.

               the explosion on July 16, 1945, at Alamogordo

military style: the explosion on 16 July 1945 at Alamogordo

               Lee's surrender to Grant on 9 April 1865 at Appomattox

7. Ordinal numbers are not used in full dates, even though the numbers may be pronounced as ordinals. Ordinals may be used, however, for a date without an accompanying year, and they are always used when preceded in a date by the word *the*.

    December 4, 1829
    on December 4th   *or*   on December 4
    on the 4th of December

8. Commas are usually omitted from dates that include the month and year but not the day. Alternatively, writers sometimes insert the word *of* between month and year.

in November 1805
back in January of 1981

9. Once a numerical date has been given, a reference to a related date may be written out.

After the meeting on June 6 the conventioneers left for home, and by the seventh the hotel was virtually empty.

10. All-figure dating, such as 6-8-95 or 6/8/95, is inappropriate except in informal correspondence. For some readers, it may also create a problem of ambiguity; the examples above may mean either June 8, 1995, or (especially in Britain and many other countries) August 6, 1995.

11. References to specific centuries are often written out, although they may be expressed in figures, especially when they form the first element of a compound modifier.

the nineteenth century
a sixteenth-century painting
but also   a 16th-century painting

12. In general correspondence, the name of a specific decade often takes a short form. Although many writers place an apostrophe before the shortened word and a few capitalize it, both the apostrophe and the capitalization are often omitted when the context clearly indicates that a date is being referred to.

in the turbulent seventies
> *but also*

back in the 'forties
in the early Fifties

13. The name of a specific decade is often expressed in numerals, usually in plural form. (For more on the formation of plural numbers, see paragraphs 14–15 on page 187.) The figure may be shortened with an apostrophe to indicate the missing numerals, but any sequence of such numbers should be styled consistently. (For more on this use of the apostrophe, see paragraph 5 on pages 4–5.)

the 1950s and 1960s   *or*   the '50s and '60s
> *but not*

the 1950s and '60s   *or*   the '50's and '60's

14. Era designations precede or follow words that specify centuries or numerals that specify years. Era designations are unspaced and are nearly always abbreviated; they are usually typed as regular capitals and typeset as small capitals, and they may or may not be punctuated with periods. Any date that is given without an era designation or context is understood to mean A.D. The two most common abbreviations are B.C. (before Christ) and A.D. (*anno Domini*, "in the year of our Lord"). The abbreviation B.C. is placed after the date, while A.D. is usually placed before the date but after a century designation.

1792–1750 B.C.

between 600 and 400 B.C.

from the fifth or fourth millennium to c. 250 B.C.

35,000 B.C.

between 7 B.C. and A.D. 22

c. A.D. 1100

the second century A.D.

the seventeenth century

15. Less commonly used era designations include A.H. (*anno Hegirae*, "in the year of [Muhammad's] Hegira," or *anno Hebraico*, "in the Hebrew year"); B.C.E. (before the common era; a synonym for B.C.); C.E. (of the common era; a synonym for A.D.); and B.P. (before the present; often used by geologists and archeologists, with or without the word *year*). The abbreviation A.H. in both its meanings is usually placed before the year number, while B.C.E., C.E., and B.P. are placed after it.

the tenth of Muharram, A.H. 61 (October 10, A.D. 680)

the first century A.H.

from the first century B.C.E. to the fourth century C.E.

63 B.C.E.

the year 200 C.E.

5,000 years B.P

two million years B.P.

Degrees of Temperature and Arc

16. In technical writing, quantities expressed in degrees are generally written as a numeral followed by the degree symbol (°). In the Kelvin scale, however, neither the word *degree* nor the symbol is used with the figure.

> a 45° angle
> 6°40'10"N
> 32° F
> 0° C
> Absolute zero is zero kelvins or 0 K.

17. In general writing, the quantity expressed in degrees may or may not be written out. A figure is usually followed by the degree symbol or the word *degree;* a written-out number is always followed by the word *degree.*

> latitude 43°19"N
> latitude 43 degrees N
> a difference of 43 degrees latitude
> The temperature has risen thirty degrees since this morning.

Enumerations and Outlines

18. Both run-in and vertical lists are often numbered. In run-in enumerations—that is, lists that form part of a normal-looking sentence—each item is preceded by a number (or an italicized letter) enclosed in parentheses. The items in the list are separated by commas if the items are brief and have little or no internal punctuation; if the items are complex, they are separated by semicolons. The entire list is introduced by a colon if it is preceded by a full clause.

We feel that she should (1) increase her administrative skills, (2) pursue additional professional education, and (3) increase her production.

The oldest and most basic word-processing systems consist of the following: (*a*) a typewriter for keyboarding information, (*b*) a console to house the storage medium, and (*c*) the medium itself.

The vendor of your system should (1) instruct you in the care and maintenance of your system; (2) offer regularly scheduled maintenance to ensure that the system is clean, with lubrication and replacement of parts as necessary; and (3) respond promptly to service calls.

19. In vertical enumerations, the numbers are usually followed by a period. Each item begins its own line, which is either flush left or indented. Run-over lines are usually aligned with the first word that follows the number, and figures are aligned on the periods that follow them. Each item on the list is usually capitalized if the items are syntactically independent of the words that introduce them; however, lowercase letters for such items are also fairly common. The items do not end with periods unless at least one of the items is a complete sentence, in which case a period follows each item. Items that are syntactically dependent on the words that introduce them begin with a lowercase letter and carry the same punctuation marks that they would if they were a run-in series in a sentence.

Required skills include the following:

1. Shorthand
2. Typing
3. Transcription

To type a three-column table, follow this procedure:

1. Clear tab stops.
2. Remove margin stops.
3. Determine precise center of the page. Set a tab stop at center.

The vendor of your system should

1. instruct you in the care and maintenance of your system;
2. offer regularly scheduled maintenance to ensure that the system is clean, with lubrication and replacement parts as necessary; and
3. respond promptly to service calls.

20. Outlines make use of Roman numerals, Arabic numerals, and letters.

    I. Editorial tasks
       A. Manuscript editing
       B. Author contact
          1. Authors already under contract
          2. New authors
   II. Production responsibilities
       A. Scheduling
          1. Composition
          2. Printing and binding
       B. Cost estimates and bids
          1. Composition
          2. Printing and binding

Fractions and Decimal Fractions

21. In running text, fractions standing alone are usually written out. Common fractions used as nouns are usually written as open compounds, but when they are used as modifiers they are usually hyphenated. (For more on written-out fractions, see paragraph 5 on page 183.)

> two thirds of the paint
> a two-thirds vote
> three thirty-seconds
> seventy-two hundredths
> one one-hundredth

22. Mixed fractions (fractions with a whole number, such as $3\frac{1}{2}$) and fractions that form part of a unit modifier are expressed in figures in running text. A *-th* is not added to a figure fraction.

> waiting $2\frac{1}{2}$ hours
> $1\frac{1}{4}$ million population
> a $\frac{7}{8}$-mile course
> a $2\frac{1}{2}$-kilometer race

When mixed fractions are typed or keyboarded a space is left between the whole number and the fraction. The space is closed up when the number is set in type. Fractions that are not on the keyboard may be made up by typing the numerator, a slash, and the denominator in succession without spacing.

> waiting 2 3/4 hours   a 7/8-mile course

23. Fractions used with units of measurement are expressed in figures.

$\frac{1}{10}$ km $\qquad\qquad$ $\frac{1}{4}$ mile

24. Decimal fractions are always set as figures. In technical writing, a zero is placed to the left of the decimal point when the fraction is less than a whole number. In general writing, the zero is usually omitted. A comma is never inserted in the numbers following a decimal point.

> An example of a pure decimal fraction is 0.375, while 1.402 is classified as a mixed decimal fraction.
> 0.142857
> 0.2 g
> received 0.1 mg/kg diazepam IV
> > *but*
> a .22-caliber rifle

25. Fractions and decimal fractions are usually not mixed in a text.

> 5$\frac{1}{2}$ lb. and 2$\frac{1}{5}$ oz.   *or*   5.5 lb. and 2.2 oz.
> > *but not*
> 5$\frac{1}{2}$ lb. and 2.2 oz.

Money

26. Sums of money are expressed in words or figures, as described in paragraphs 1–2 on pages 175–76. If the sum can be expressed in one or two words, it is usually written out in running text. But if several sums are mentioned in the sentence or paragraph, all are usually expressed as figures. When the amount is written out, the unit of currency is also written out. If the sum is expressed in figures, the symbol of the currency unit is used, with no space between it and the numerals.

> Fifty dollars was stolen from my wallet.
> The price of a nickel candy bar seems to have risen to more like sixty cents.
> The shop charges $67.50 for our hand-knit sweaters.
> My change came to 87¢.
> We paid $175,000 for the house.

27. Monetary units of mixed dollars-and-cents amounts are expressed in figures.

> $16.75
> $307.02
> $1.95

28. Even-dollar amounts are often expressed in figures without a decimal point and zeros. But when even-dollar amounts appear near amounts that include dollars and cents, the decimal point and zeros are usually added for consistency. The dollar sign is repeated before each amount in a series or inclusive range; the word *dollar* may or may not be repeated.

> The price of the book rose from $7.95 in 1970 to $8.00 in 1971 and then to $8.50 in 1972.
> The bids were eighty, ninety, and one hundred dollars.

or
The bids were eighty dollars, ninety dollars, and one hundred dollars.

29. Sums of money given in round units of millions or above are usually expressed in a combination of figures and words, either with a dollar sign or with the word *dollars*. (For more on round numbers, see paragraphs 7–8 on pages 178–79.)

60 million dollars
a $10 million building program
$4.5 billion

30. In legal documents a sum of money is usually written out fully, with the corresponding figures in parentheses immediately following.

twenty-five thousand dollars ($25,000)

Percentages

31. In technical writing, specific percentages are written as figure plus symbol %. In general correspondence, the percentage number may be expressed as a figure or spelled out. The word *percent* rather than the symbol is used in nonscientific texts.

technical: 15%
    13.5%
general: 15 percent
    87.2 percent
    Twenty-five percent of the office staff was out with the flu.
    a four percent increase

32. The word *percentage* or *percent,* used as a noun without an adjacent numeral, should never be replaced by a percent sign.

> Only a small percentage of the staff objected to the smoking ban.

33. In a series or unit combination, the percent sign should be included with all numbers, even if one of the numbers is zero.

> a variation of 0% to 10%

Proper Names

34. Numbers in the names of religious organizations and churches are usually written out in ordinal form. Names of specific governmental bodies may include ordinals, and these are written out if they are one hundred or below.

> Third Congregational Church
> Seventh-Day Adventists
> Third Reich
> First Continental Congress

35. Names of electoral, judicial, and military units may include ordinal numbers that precede the noun. Numbers of one hundred or below are usually written out.

> First Congressional District
> Twelfth Precinct
> Ninety-eighth Congress *or* 98th Congress
> Court of Appeals for the Third Circuit
> United States Eighth Army

36. Local branches of labor unions and fraternal organizations are generally identified by a numeral usually placed after the name.

> International Brotherhood of Electrical
>   Workers Local 42
> Elks Lodge No. 61
> Local 98 Operating Engineers

Ratios

37. Ratios expressed in figures use a colon, a hyphen, a slash, or the word *to* to indicate comparison. Ratios expressed in words use a hyphen or the word *to*.

> a 3:1 chance
> a 6-1 vote
> 22.4 mi/gal
> odds of 100 to 1
> a fifty-fifty chance
> a ratio of ten to four

Serial Numbers and Other Numerals

38. Figures are used to refer to things that are numbered serially, such as chapter and page numbers, addresses, years, policy and contract numbers, and so forth.

> pages 420–515
> vol. 5, p. 202
> column 2
> Serial No. 5274
> Permit No. 63709

39. Figures are also used to express stock-market quotations, mathematical calculations, scores, and tabulations.

> 3⅛ percent bonds
> $3 \times 15 = 45$
> won by a score of 8 to 2
> the tally: 322 ayes, 80 nays

Time of Day

40. In running text, the time of day is usually spelled out when expressed in even, half, or quarter hours.

> Quitting time is four-thirty.
> The meeting should be over by half past eleven.
> We should arrive at a quarter past five.

41. The time of day is also usually spelled out when it is followed by the contraction *o'clock* or when *o'clock* is understood.

> He should be here by four at the latest.
> My appointment is at eleven o'clock.
> *or* My appointment is at 11 o'clock.

42. Figures are used to specify a precise time.

> The meeting is scheduled for 9:15 in the morning.
> Her plane is due at 3:05 this afternoon.
> The program starts at 8:30 in the evening.

43. Figures are also written when the time of day is used with the abbreviations *a.m. (ante meri-*

diem) and *p.m. (post meridiem)*. The lowercase styling for these abbreviations is most common, but small capital letters are also frequently used. These abbreviations should not be used with the words *morning* or *evening* or the word *o'clock*.

> 8:30 a.m. *or* 8:30 A.M.
> 10:30 p.m. *or* 10:30 P.M.
> 8 a.m. *or* 8 A.M.
>   *but*
> 9:15 in the morning
> 11:00 in the evening
> nine o'clock

When twelve o'clock is written, it is helpful to add the designation *midnight* or *noon* rather than *a.m.* or *p.m.*

> twelve o'clock (midnight)
> twelve o'clock (noon)

44. For consistency, even-hour times should be written with a colon and two zeros when used in a series or pairing with any odd-hour times.

> He came at 7:00 and left at 9:45.

45. The 24-hour clock system—also called military time—uses no punctuation and is expressed without the use of *a.m., p.m.,* or *o'clock*; the word *hours* sometimes replaces them.

> from 0930 to 1100
> at 1600 hours

Units of Measurement

46. Numbers used with units of measurement are treated according to the basic conventions explained in the first part of this chapter. However, in some cases writers achieve greater clarity by writing out all numbers (even those below ten) that express quantities of physical measurement as numerals.

> The car was traveling in excess of 80 miles an hour.
>
> The old volume weighed three pounds and was difficult to hold in a reading position.
>
> *but also in some general texts*
>
> 3 hours, 25 minutes
>
> saw 18 eagles in 12 minutes
>
> a 6-pound hammer
>
> weighed 3 pounds, 5 ounces

47. When units of measurement are written as abbreviations or symbols, the adjacent numbers are always figures.

> 6 cm   67.6 fl oz
>
> 1 mm   4'
>
> $4.25   98.6°

48. When two or more quantities are expressed, as in ranges or dimensions or series, an accompanying symbol is usually repeated with each figure.

> 4″ × 6″ cards
>
> temperature on successive days of 30°, 55°, 43°, and 58°
>
> $400–$500

Chapter 6

Grammar and Composition

No guide to effective communication can ignore the basic components of writing: the word, the phrase, the clause, the sentence, and the paragraph. Each of these increasingly complex units contributes to the expression of a writer's ideas. Basic to all of them is the word.

Words have traditionally been classified into eight parts of speech: adjective, adverb, conjunction, interjection, noun, preposition, pronoun, and verb. This classification is based mainly on a word's inflectional features (or changes in form), its grammatical functions, and its position within a sentence. On the following pages, the parts of speech are discussed briefly in alphabetical order.

Adjective

An adjective is a word that describes or modifies the meaning of a noun. Adjectives serve to point out a quality of a thing named, indicate its quantity or extent, or specify a thing as distinct from something else.

Adjectives are often classified by the ways in which they modify or limit the meaning of a noun. The following paragraphs describe, in alphabetical order, the various types of adjectives and also outline situations involving adjectives that are sometimes troublesome for writers.

Absolute Adjectives

1. Some adjectives (such as *prior, maximum, optimum, minimum,* and *first*) normally cannot be used comparatively (see paragraphs 4 and 5 below), because they represent ultimate conditions. These adjectives are called *absolute* (or *nongradable*) *adjectives*. Some writers are careful to modify these adjectives with adverbs such as *almost, near,* or *nearly*, rather than *least, less, more, most,* or *very*.

> an *almost fatal* dose
> at *near maximum* capacity
> a *more nearly perfect* likeness

However, many writers do compare and qualify this type of adjective in order to show connotations and shades of meaning they consider less than absolute.

> a *more perfect* union
> a *less complete* account

When in doubt about the comparability of an absolute adjective, check the definitions and examples of usage given in a dictionary.

Adjective/Noun Agreement

2. The number (singular or plural) of a demonstrative adjective *(this, that, these, those)* should agree with that of the noun it modifies. (See also paragraph 11 below.)

> *these kinds* of typewriters
>   *not   these kind* of typewriters
> *those sorts* of jobs   *not   those sort* of jobs
> *this type* of person   *not   these type* of people

Articles

3. An article is one of three words *(a, an,* and *the)* that are used with nouns to limit or give definiteness to the application of a noun.

Compared with Adverbs

4. Both adjectives and adverbs describe or modify other words; however, adjectives can only modify nouns, while adverbs can modify

verbs, adverbs, and adjectives. For more on the differences between adjectives and adverbs, see paragraph 20 on pages 213–14 and paragraphs 4–6 on pages 216–17.

Comparison of Adjectives

5. A *gradable* adjective can indicate degrees of comparison (positive, comparative, superlative) by the addition of the endings *-er* and *-est* to the base word; the addition of *more, most, less,* and *least* before the base word; or the use of irregular forms.

positive	comparative	superlative
clean	cleaner	cleanest
meaningful	less meaningful	least meaningful
bad	worse	worst

6. The comparative degree is used to show that the thing being modified has more (or less) of a particular quality than the one or ones to which it is being compared. The superlative degree is used to show that the thing being modified has the most (or least) of a quality out of all those things to which it is being compared. The superlative degree is used when there are more than two things being compared.

comparative	superlative
prices *higher* than those elsewhere	the *highest* price in the area
a *better* report than our last one	the *best* report so far
the *more expensive* of the two methods	the *most expensive* of the three methods

7. The comparatives and superlatives of one-syllable adjectives are usually formed by adding *-er* and *-est* to the base word. The comparatives and superlatives of adjectives with more than two syllables are formed by adding *more, most, less,* and *least* before the base word. The comparatives and superlatives of two-syllable adjectives are formed by either adding *-er* and *-est* to the base word or using *more, most, less,* and *least* before the base word. When in doubt about the inflection of a particular adjective, consult a dictionary, which will show irregular forms. (If none are shown, the inflection is normal.)

positive	comparative	superlative
big	bigger	biggest
narrow	narrower	narrowest
complex	more complex	most complex
concise	less concise	least concise
important	more important	most important

8. Some adjectives are ordinarily not compared, because they are felt to represent ultimate conditions (see paragraph 1 above).

Coordinate Adjectives

9. Adjectives that share equal relationships to the nouns they modify are called *coordinate adjectives* and are separated from each other by commas.

a *concise, coherent* essay

a *soft, flickering* light

10. When the first of two adjectives modifies the noun plus the second adjective, the result is a pair of *noncoordinate adjectives*. Such adjectives are not separated by commas.

> a *low monthly* fee
> the *first warm* day

Demonstrative Adjectives

11. The demonstrative adjective *this* or *that* points to what it modifies in order to distinguish it from others. *This* and *that* are the only two adjectives with plural forms: *these* and *those*. (See also paragraph 2 above.)

Descriptive Adjectives

12. A descriptive adjective describes something or indicates a quality, kind, or condition.

> a *brave* soldier
> a *new* dress
> a *sick* pony

Double Comparisons

13. Double comparisons should not be used.

> an *easier* method   *not*   a *more easier* method
> the *easiest* solution   *not*   the *most easiest* solution

Incomplete or Understood Comparisons

14. Some comparisons are left incomplete because the context clearly implies the comparison. However, the use of incomplete comparisons, especially for making vague claims of superiority such as commonly appear in advertising, is often considered careless or illogical in formal writing.

> *Older* Americans vote in *larger* numbers.
> Get *better* buys here!
> We have *lower* prices.

Indefinite Adjectives

15. An indefinite adjective designates unidentified or not immediately identifiable persons or things.

> *some* children
> *other* hotels

Interrogative Adjectives

16. Interrogative adjectives are used in asking questions.

> *Whose* office is this?
> *Which* book do you want?

Nouns Used as Adjectives

17. Nouns are frequently used to describe other nouns, and in this way they act like adjectives. For more on the use of nouns as modifiers, see paragraph 7 on pages 232–33 and paragraphs 25–26 on page 139.

Placement within a Sentence

18. Adjectives may occur in the following positions within sentences: (1) preceding the

nouns they modify, (2) following the nouns they modify, (3) following the verb *to be* (*am, is, are, was, were,* etc.) and other linking verbs in the predicate-adjective position, and (4) following some transitive verbs used in the passive voice.

> the *black* hat
> a *dark, shabby* coat
> painted the room *blue*
> a hat that is *black*
> while I felt *sick*
> a room that was painted *blue*
> passengers found *dead* at the crash site

Possessive Adjectives

19. A possessive adjective is the possessive form of a personal pronoun.

> *her* idea
> *my* car
> *our* paintings

Predicate Adjectives

20. A predicate adjective modifies the subject of a linking verb (such as *be, become, feel, taste, smell, seem*) which it follows.

> She is *happy* with the outcome.
> The milk tastes *sour*.
> The student seems *puzzled*.

Because some linking verbs (such as *feel, look, smell, taste*) can also function as active verbs, which can in turn be modified by adverbs, writers are sometimes confused over whether they should use the adverbial or adjectival form of a modifier after the verb. The answer is that an adjective is used if the subject of the sentence is being modified. If the verb is being modified, an adverb is used. (For more examples, see paragraph 5 on pages 216–17.)

adjective: Your memo looks *good.*
              The colors feel *right.*
              The engine smells *hot.*

adverb: They looked *quickly* at each item.
             He felt *immediately* for his wallet.
             She smelled the food *carefully* for spoilage.

Proper Adjectives

21. A proper adjective is derived from a proper noun and is usually capitalized.

    Victorian furniture
    a *Puerto Rican* product.
    Keynesian economics

Relative Adjectives

22. A relative adjective *(which, that, who, whom, whose, where)* introduces an adjectival clause or a clause that functions as a noun.

    at the April conference, by *which* time the report should be finished
    not knowing *whose* lead she should follow

Adverb

An adverb is a word or combination of words that typically serves as a modifier of a verb, an adjective, another adverb, a preposition, a phrase, a clause, or a sentence and expresses some relation of manner or quality, place, time, degree, number, cause, opposition, affirmation, or denial. Because of its many roles, the adverb can be one of the most confusing parts of speech.

Most adverbs are adjectives with an *-ly* ending added (*actually, congenially, madly, really*). There are many exceptions to this pattern, however. Adverbs based on adjectives ending in *-ly* (*cowardly, early, daily*) do not include an additional *-ly* ending but take the same form as the adjective. In addition, some adverbs do not end in *-ly* (*again, now, quite, too*).

Adverbs answer such questions as: *when?* ("Please reply *at once*"), *how long?* ("This is taking *forever*"), *where?* ("She works *there*"), *in what direction?* ("Move the lever *upward*"), *how?* ("They moved *quickly*"), and *to what degree?* ("It was *very* popular").

Basic Uses

1. Adverbs modify verbs, adjectives, and other adverbs.

> She *carefully* studied the balance sheet.
> She gave the balance sheet *very* careful study.
> She studied the balance sheet *very* carefully.

2. Conjunctive adverbs join clauses or link sentences. (For more on this use of adverbs, see paragraphs 13–16 on pages 226–28.)

> You're welcome to join our hiking club; *however,* the hikes are strenuous.
>
> He thoroughly enjoyed the opera. *Indeed,* he was fascinated by the soprano.

3. In addition, adverbs may be essential elements of two-word verbs.

> Our staff will work *up* the specifications.
>
> We can farm them *out* later.

Compared with Adjectives

4. Adverbs but not adjectives modify action verbs.

> *not:*   He answered very *harsh.*
>
> *instead:* He answered very *harshly.*

5. A word referring to the subject of a sentence and occurring after a linking verb normally is an adjective rather than an adverb. (For more examples, see paragraph 20 on page 213.)

> *not:*   He looks *badly* these days.
>
>   The letter sounded *strongly.*
>
> *instead:* He looks *bad* these days.
>
>   The letter sounded *strong.*
>
> *and also:* He looks *good* these days.
>
>   He looks *well* these days.

In the last two examples, either *good* or *well* is acceptable, because both words are here functioning as adjectives in the sense of "healthy."

6. Adverbs but not adjectives modify adjectives and other adverbs.

not: She looked *dreadful* tired.
instead: She looked *dreadfully* tired.

Comparison of Adverbs

7. Most adverbs have three different forms to indicate degrees of comparison: positive, comparative, and superlative. The *positive* form is the base word itself (*quickly, loudly, near*). The *comparative* form is usually shown by the addition of *more* or *less* before the base word (*more quickly, less quickly*). The *superlative* form is usually shown by the addition of *most* or *least* (*most quickly, least quickly*). However, a few adverbs (such as *fast, slow, loud, soft, early, late,* and *near*) may also be compared by the addition of the endings *-er* and *-est* to the base word (*near, nearer, nearest*). For an explanation of the uses of the comparative and superlative forms, see paragraphs 5–6 on page 209.

8. As a general rule, one-syllable adverbs add the *-er* and *-est* endings to show comparison. Adverbs of three or more syllables use *more/ most* and *less/least*. Two-syllable adverbs take one form or the other. (For more details, see paragraph 7 on page 210.)

positive	comparative	superlative
fast	faster	fastest
easy	easier	easiest
madly	more madly	most madly
happily	more happily	most happily

9. Some adverbs (such as *quite* and *very*) cannot be compared.

Double Negatives and Similar Cases

10. A combination of two adverbs with negative meaning (such as *not, hardly, never,* and *scarcely*) to express a single negative idea should be avoided.

not: We *cannot* see *hardly* any reason to buy this product.

instead: We *cannot* see any reason to buy this product.

We can see *hardly* any reason to buy this product.

Emphasis

11. Adverbs such as *just* and *only* are often used to emphasize other words. Various emphases can result from the positioning of an adverb in a sentence.

He *just* nodded to me as he passed.

He nodded to me *just* as he passed.

12. In some positions and contexts, these adverbs can be ambiguous.

They will *only* tell it to you.

It is not clear whether this means that they will only tell it—that is, not put it in writing—or that they will tell no one else. If the latter interpretation is intended, a slight shift of position would remove the uncertainty.

They will tell it *only* to you.

Placement within a Sentence

13. Adverbs are generally positioned as close as possible to the words they modify, if such a position will not result in misinterpretation.

unclear: A project that the board would support *completely* occupied her thinking.

Here it is unclear whether the writer means "would support completely" or "completely occupied her thinking." The adverb may be moved to another position, or the sentence may be rewritten.

clear: A project that the board would *completely* support occupied her thinking.

Her thinking was *completely* occupied with a project that the board would support.

14. When an adverb separates *to* from the verbal element of an infinitive ("hope to really start"), the result is called a *split infinitive*. For a discussion of split infinitives, see paragraph 35 on pages 265–66.

15. Adverbs sometimes modify an entire sentence rather than a specific word or phrase within the sentence. Such adverbs are referred to as *sentence adverbs,* and their position can vary.

> *Fortunately* they had already placed their order.
> They *fortunately* had already placed their order.
> They had already placed their order, *fortunately.*

Relative Adverbs

16. Relative adverbs (such as *when, where, why*) introduce subordinate clauses. (For more on subordinate clauses, see the section beginning on page 270.)

> They met at a time *when* prospects were good.
> I went into the room *where* they were sitting.
> Everyone knows the reason *why* she did it.

Conjunction

A conjunction is a word or phrase that joins together words, phrases, clauses, or sentences. Conjunctions may occur in many different positions in a sentence. There are three main types of conjunctions: *coordinating, correlative,* and *subordinating.* In addition, there are transitional adverbs and adverbial phrases called *conjunctive adverbs.* These function as conjunctions even though they are customarily classified as adverbs. A definition and discussion of the three types of conjunctions and of conjunctive adverbs follows.

Coordinating Conjunctions

1. Coordinating conjunctions (such as *and, because, but, for, or, nor, since, so,* and *yet*) join to-

gether grammatical elements of equal weight. The elements may be words, phrases, subordinate clauses, main clauses, or complete sentences. Coordinating conjunctions are used to join similar elements, to exclude or contrast, to offer alternatives, to propose reasons or grounds, or to specify a result.

joining similar elements:	She ordered pencils, pens, *and* erasers.
	Sales were slow, *and* they showed no sign of improvement.
excluding or contrasting:	He is a brilliant *but* arrogant man.
	They offered a promising plan, *but* it had not yet been tested.
alternative:	She can wait here *or* go on ahead.
reason or grounds:	The report is useless, *for* its information is no longer current.
result:	His diction is excellent, *so* every word is clear.

2. A comma is used before a coordinating conjunction linking coordinate clauses, especially when these clauses are lengthy. (For more on the use of commas between clauses, see paragraphs 1–4 on pages 14–16.)

We encourage applications from all interested students, *but* we do have high academic standards that the successful applicant must meet.

3. Coordinating conjunctions should link equal grammatical elements—for example, adjec-

tives with other adjectives, nouns with other nouns, participles with other participles, clauses with other equal-ranking clauses, and so on. Combining unequal grammatical elements may result in unbalanced sentences.

unbalanced: Having become disgusted *and* because he was tired, he left the meeting.

balanced: Because he was tired *and* disgusted, he left the meeting.

Having become tired *and* disgusted, he left the meeting.

4. Coordinating conjunctions should not be used to string together a long series of elements, regardless of their grammatical equality.

loose: We have sustained enormous losses in this division, *and* we have realized practically no profits even though the sales figures indicate last-quarter gains, *and* we are therefore reorganizing the entire management structure as well as cutting back on personnel.

tightened: Because this division has sustained enormous losses and has realized only insignificant profits even with its last-quarter sales gains, we are totally reorganizing its management and cutting back on personnel.

5. The choice of the right coordinating conjunction is important: the right word will pinpoint the writer's true meaning and intent and will emphasize the most relevant idea or point of

the sentence. The following three sentences show increasingly stronger degrees of contrast through the use of different conjunctions:

> He works hard *and* doesn't progress.
> He works hard *but* doesn't progress.
> He works hard, *yet* he doesn't progress.

6. The coordinating conjunction *and/or* linking two elements of a compound subject often poses a problem: should the verb that follows be singular or plural? A subject consisting of singular nouns connected by *and/or* may be considered singular or plural, depending on the meaning of the sentence.

singular: All loss *and/or* damage [one or the other and possibly both] *is* to be the responsibility of the sender.

plural: John R. Westlake *and/or* Maria A. Artandi *are* hereby appointed as the executors of my estate. [Both executors are to act, or either of them is to act if the other dies or is incapacitated.]

Correlative Conjunctions

7. Correlative conjunctions are coordinating conjunctions that are used in pairs, although they are not placed adjacent to one another. Correlative conjunctions are used to link alternatives and equal elements.

> *Either* you go *or* you stay.
> He had *neither* looks *nor* wit.

> *Both* typist *and* writer should understand the rules of punctuation.
>
> *Not only* was there inflation, *but* there was *also* unemployment.

8. Because they link equal grammatical elements, correlative conjunctions should be placed as close as possible to the elements they join. What follows *either* should be parallel to what follows *or;* for example, if a verb immediately follows one of these words, a verb must immediately follow the other.

> *misplaced:*   *Either* I must send a fax *or* make a long-distance call.
>
> *repositioned:*   I must *either* send a fax *or* make a long-distance call.

9. The negative counterpart to *either ... or* is *neither ... nor.* The conjunction *or* should not be substituted for *nor,* because its substitution will destroy the negative parallelism. However, *or* may occur in combination with *no.*

> *not:*   He received *neither* a promotion *or* a raise.
>
> *instead:*   He received *neither* a promotion *nor* a raise.
>
> He received *no* promotion *or* raise.

Subordinating Conjunctions

10. Subordinating conjunctions join a subordinate or dependent clause to a main clause. They are used to express cause, condition or concession, manner, purpose or result, time, place or circumstance, and alternative conditions or possibilities.

cause:	*Because* she learns quickly, she is doing well in her new job.
condition or concession:	Don't call *unless* you are coming.
manner:	He looks *as though* he is ill.
	We'll do it *however* you tell us to.
purpose or result:	She routes the mail early *so that* they can read it.
time:	She kept meetings to a minimum *when* she was president.
place or cir-cumstance:	I don't know *where* he went.
	He tries to help out *wherever* it is possible.
conditions or possibilities:	It was hard to decide *whether* I should go or stay.

11. The subordinating conjunction *that* introduces several kinds of subordinate clauses, including those used as noun equivalents (such as a subject or an object of a verb or as a predicate nominative).

> Yesterday I learned *that* he has been sick for over a week.

12. In introducing subordinate clauses, subordinating conjunctions de-emphasize less important ideas in favor of more important ideas. The writer should take care that the point to be emphasized is in the main clause and that the points of less importance are subordinated.

We were just coming out of the door *when* the building burst into flames.

As we were coming out of the door, the building burst into flames.

Conjunctive Adverbs

13. Conjunctive adverbs are transitional adverbs and adverbial phrases that express relationships between two independent units (such as two main clauses, two complete sentences, or two or more paragraphs). Though classed as adverbs, they function as conjunctions when they are used as connectives. Some common conjunctive adverbs are listed below.

accordingly	hence	namely
also	however	nevertheless
besides	in addition	otherwise
consequently	indeed	still
finally	in fact	then
first	meanwhile	therefore
furthermore	moreover	thus

14. Conjunctive adverbs are used to express addition, to add emphasis, to express contrast or discrimination, to introduce illustrations or elaborations, to express or introduce conclusions or results, or to order phrases or clauses in terms of time, space, or priority.

addition: This employee deserves a substantial raise; *furthermore,* she should be promoted.

emphasis: He is brilliant; *indeed,* he is a genius.

contrast or discrimination:	The major responsibility lies with the partners; *nevertheless,* associates should be competent in decision-making.
illustrations or elaborations:	Losses were due to several negative factors; *namely,* inflation, foreign competition, and restrictive government regulation.
conclusions or results:	Government overregulation in that country has reached a prohibitive level. *Thus,* we are phasing out all of our operations there.
time, space, or priority:	*First,* we can remind them that their account is long overdue; *second,* we can say that we must consider consulting our attorneys if they do not meet their obligation.

15. Conjunctive adverbs are usually placed at the beginning of a clause or sentence. When they are placed later in the clause or sentence, they receive additional emphasis.

> The overdue shipment arrived this morning; *however,* we must point out that it was incomplete.
>
> The overdue shipment arrived this morning; we must point out, *however,* that it was incomplete.

16. A semicolon is used before a conjunctive adverb connecting two main clauses. Using a comma with conjunctive adverbs leads to a problem known as *comma fault*. (For more on comma fault and punctuation between main clauses, see paragraphs 1–4 on pages 14–16 and paragraph 5 on page 69.)

comma fault: The company had flexible hours, *however* its employees were expected to abide by their selected arrival and departure times.

corrected: The company had flexible hours; *however*, its employees were expected to abide by their selected arrival and departure times.

Interjection

Interjections are exclamatory or interrupting words or phrases that express an emotion. Interjections are usually independent clauses that lack grammatical connection with the rest of the sentence. They often stand alone.

1. Interjections may be stressed or ejaculatory words, phrases, or even short sentences.

Absurd!   Get out!

No, no!   Not now!

2. Interjections may also be so-called "sound" words, such as those representing shouts, hisses, or cries.

Shh! The meeting has begun.

Pssst! Come over here.

Ouch! That hurts.

Ugh! What a horrible flavor.

3. Emphatic interjections expressing forceful emotions use exclamation points. Mildly stressed words or sentences may be punctuated with commas and periods.

Fire!

What an awful time we had!

Ah, that's my idea of a terrific beer.

Well, well, so that's their story now.

Oh, you're probably right.

4. Interjections should be sparingly used, and then only to signal genuine emotion or for strong emphasis.

Noun

A noun is the name of something (such as a person, animal, place, object, quality, concept, or action). Nouns are used as the subject or object of a verb, the object of a preposition, the predicate after a linking verb, an appositive name, or a name in an absolute construction.

Nouns have several characteristic features. They can take a possessive form; they have number (that is, they are either singular or plural); they are often preceded by determiners (such as *a, an, the; this, that, these, those; all, every; one, two, three; his, her, their*); a few still show gender differences *(host/hostess, actor/actress)*; and many are formed by adding a suffix (such as *-ance, -ist, -ness,* or *-tion*) to a root or verb form.

Basic Uses

1. Nouns are used as subjects, direct objects, objects of prepositions, indirect objects, retained objects, predicate nominatives, objective complements, and appositives, and in direct address.

subject:	The *office* was quiet.
direct object:	He locked the *office.*
object of a preposition:	The file is in the *office.*
indirect object:	He gave his *client* the papers.
retained object:	His client was given the *papers.*
predicate nominative:	Mrs. Adams is the managing *partner.*
objective complement:	They made Mrs. Adams managing *partner.*
appositive:	Mrs. Adams, the managing *partner,* wrote that memo.
direct address:	*Mrs. Adams,* may I present Mr. Bonkowski.

Compound Nouns

2. Because English is not static and unchanging, many of its words undergo styling variations because of the changing preferences of its users. The styling of compound nouns (that is, as open, closed, or hyphenated) is espe-

cially subject to changing usage. No set of rules can cover every possible variation or combination; however, some consistent patterns of usage can be seen. For more details, see the section beginning on page 131.

Indefinite Articles with Nouns

3. Before a word or abbreviation beginning with a consonant *sound*, the article *a* is used. This is true even if the word begins with a vowel.

a door	a human
a COD package	a union
a B.A. degree	a one
a hat	a U.S. Senator

4. Before *h-* in an unstressed or lightly stressed first syllable, the article *a* is generally used, although *an* is more usual in speech whether or not the *h-* is actually pronounced. Either is acceptable in both speech and writing.

a historian   *or*   an historian
a heroic attempt   *or*   an heroic attempt
a hilarious performance   *or*   an hilarious performance

5. Before a word or abbreviation beginning with a vowel *sound*, the article *an* is used. This is true even if the word or abbreviation actually begins with a consonant.

an icicle	an nth degree
an orange	an FCC report
an unknown	an MIT professor
an honor	an Rh factor

Nominals

6. Nominals are words or groups of words that function as nouns. Adjectives, gerunds, and infinitives may act as nominals. An example of an adjective used as a noun is the word *good* in the clause "the good die young." Examples of gerunds and infinitives used as nouns are *seeing* in the clause "seeing is believing" and *to see* in the clause "to see is to believe." Noun phrases and noun clauses are also considered to be nominals. For more about gerunds and infinitives, see paragraphs 14 and 16 on pages 258–59. For information about noun phrases and noun clauses, see paragraph 4 on page 268 and paragraph 3 on page 271 respectively.

Nouns Used as Adjectives

7. Nouns are frequently used as adjectives by placing them before other nouns, as in *school board* or *office management*. When two or more nouns are frequently combined in this way, they become familiar compounds like *profit margin, money market, box lunch.* Such compounds provide useful verbal shortcuts ("office management" is shorter than "management of an office"). However, care should be

taken not to pile up so many of these noun modifiers that the reader has difficulty sorting out their meanings.

shorter but unclear: Management review copies of the Division II sales department machine parts file should be indexed.

longer but clear: Copies of the machine parts file from the Division II sales department should be indexed before being sent to management for review.

Both of these sentences could be made clearer by hyphenating the compound nouns used as adjectives. (For more about this kind of compound, see the section beginning on page 143.)

Management-review copies of the Division II sales department's machine-parts file should be indexed.

Plurals

8. The plurals of nouns are usually produced by adding *-s* or *-es* to the base word, although some nouns have irregular plurals. For more about the formation of plurals, see the section beginning on page 114.

Possessives

9. The possessives of nouns are usually formed by adding an apostrophe plus *-s* to singular nouns or just an apostrophe to plural words ending in -*s*. For more about possessives, see the section beginning on page 123.

Proper Nouns

10. Proper nouns are nouns that name a particular person, place, or thing. Proper nouns are almost always capitalized. For more about capitalizing proper nouns, see the section beginning on page 79.

Preposition

A preposition is a word that combines with a noun, pronoun, or noun equivalent (such as a phrase or clause) to form a phrase that usually acts as an adverb, adjective, or noun.

Prepositions have no inflections, number, case, gender, or identifying suffixes. They can be identified chiefly by their position within sentences and by their grammatical functions. Prepositions may be simple—that is, consisting of only one word (*against, from, near, of, on, out,* or *without*)—or compound—that is, composed of more than one element (*according to, by means of,* or *in spite of*).

Basic Uses

1. Prepositions are chiefly used to link nouns, pronouns, or noun equivalents to the rest of the sentence. A prepositional phrase usually functions as an adverb or an adjective.

She expected resistance *on* his part.

He sat down *beside* her.

Conjunctions vs. Prepositions

2. The words *after, before, but, for,* and *since* may function as either prepositions or conjunctions. Their position within the sentence identifies them as conjunctions or prepositions. Conjunctions link two words or sentence elements that have the same grammatical function. Prepositions normally precede a noun, pronoun, or noun phrase.

conjunction: I was a bit concerned *but* not panicky. [*but* links two adjectives]

preposition: I was left with nothing *but* hope. [*but* precedes a noun]

conjunction: The device conserves fuel, *for* it is battery-powered. [*for* links two clauses]

preposition: The device conserves fuel *for* residual heating. [*for* precedes a noun phrase]

Implied Prepositions

3. If two words combine idiomatically with the same preposition, that preposition need not be used after both.

We were antagonistic [*to*] and opposed *to* the whole idea.

but

We are interested *in* and anxious *for* raises.

Position

4. Prepositions may occur before nouns or pronouns ("*below* the desk," "*beside* them"), after

adjectives ("antagonistic *to*," "insufficient *in*," "symbolic *of*"), and after the verbal elements of standard verb + preposition combinations ("take *for*," "get *after*," "come *across*").

5. There is no reason why a preposition cannot end a sentence, especially when it is an element in a common verb phrase.

> His lack of organization is only one of the things I put up *with*.
> What does all this add up *to*?

Use of *Between* and *Among*

6. Despite an unfounded notion to the contrary, the preposition *between* can be used of more than two items. It is especially appropriate to denote one-to-one relationships, regardless of the number of items.

> Treaties established economic cooperation *between* nations.
> This is *between* you and me and the lamppost.

Among is more appropriate where the emphasis is on overall distribution rather than individual relationships.

> There was discontent *among* the peasants.

When *among* is automatically chosen for more than two, the results can sound strained.

> The author alternates *among* quotes, clichés, and street slang.

Pronoun

A pronoun is a word that is used as a substitute for a noun or noun equivalent, takes noun constructions, and refers to persons or things named or understood in the context. The noun or noun equivalent for which it substitutes is called the *antecedent*.

Pronouns may exhibit the following features: case (nominative, possessive, objective); number (singular, plural); person (first, second, third person); and gender (masculine, feminine, neuter). Pronouns are divided into seven major categories, each with its own function; they are described alphabetically below.

Demonstrative Pronouns

1. The words *this*, *that*, *these*, and *those* are classified as pronouns when they function as nouns. (They are classified as demonstrative adjectives when they modify nouns.) Demonstrative pronouns point out a person or thing to distinguish it from others of the same type.

   These are the best designs we've seen to date.

   Those are strong words.

2. They also distinguish between a person or thing nearby and one farther away.

   This is my desk; *that* is yours.

3. A potentially troublesome situation occurs when a demonstrative pronoun introduces a

sentence, referring back to something previously mentioned. The reference should always be clear.

unclear: The heir's hemophilia, the influence of an unprincipled faith healer on the royal family, devastating military setbacks, general strikes, mass outbreaks of typhus, and repeated crop failures contributed to the revolution. *This* influenced the course of history.

clear: The heir's hemophilia, the influence of an unprincipled faith healer on the royal family, devastating military setbacks, general strikes, mass outbreaks of typhus, and repeated crop failures—all these factors contributed to the revolution and thus influenced the course of history.

4. When demonstrative pronouns are used with the words *kind/sort/type* + *of* + noun, they should agree in number with both nouns.

not: We want *these kind* of *pencils.*

instead: We want *this kind* of *pencil.*

We want *these kinds* of *pencils.*

Indefinite Pronouns

5. Indefinite pronouns designate an unidentified or not immediately identifiable person or thing. They are chiefly used as third-person references and do not distinguish gender. Examples of indefinite pronouns are listed below.

all	either	none
another	everybody	no one
any	everyone	one
anybody	everything	other
anyone	few	several
anything	many	some
both	much	somebody
each	neither	someone
each one	nobody	something

6. Indefinite pronouns should agree in number with their verbs. The following are singular and take singular verbs: *another, anything, each one, everything, much, nobody, no one, one, other, someone, something.*

   Much is being done.
   No one wants to go.

7. The indefinite pronouns *both, few, many, several,* and a few others are plural and take plural verbs.

   Many were called; *few were* chosen.

8. Some indefinite pronouns (such as *all, any, none, some*) present problems because they may be either singular or plural, depending on whether they are used with mass nouns or count nouns. (A *mass noun* identifies something not ordinarily thought of in terms of countable elements; a *count noun* identifies things that can be counted.)

with mass noun: *All* of the *property is* entailed.
None of the *ink was* erasable.
Some of the *sky was* visible.

with count noun: *All* of our *bases are* covered.
None of the *clerks were* available.
Some of the *stars were* visible.

9. The pronouns *anybody, anyone, everybody, everyone, somebody, nobody,* and *no one* are singular in form and as such logically take singular verbs. However, because of the plural aspect of their meaning, plural pronoun references to them are common in informal speech.

> I knew *everybody* by *their* first names.
> Don't tell *anyone; they* might spread the rumor.

Even in more formal contexts, such plural pronoun references are used increasingly, especially to avoid sexism in language. (For more about avoiding sexism in the use of personal pronouns, see paragraph 23 on page 246.)

> We called *everyone* by *their* first *names* [rather than "his first name"].

10. Sometimes an apparently singular indefinite pronoun may take a plural verb if the context makes it seem plural. The following two sentences illustrate how a singular indefinite pronoun may take either a singular or a plural verb, depending on how the writer interprets the pronoun *either* (or *neither*):

> *Either* [*Neither*] of these pronunciations *is* acceptable.

Either [*Neither*] of these pronunciations *are* acceptable.

The normal choice of verb would be *is*, because the subject of the sentence is the singular pronoun. However, the plural word *pronunciations*, together with the possibility of interpreting *either* and *neither* to refer alternatively to one or both, permits the writer to choose either a singular or a plural verb.

11. The indefinite pronouns *any* and *anyone* are usually followed by *other(s)* or *else* in a comparison of two individuals in the same class.

    not: Helen has more seniority than *anyone* in the firm.

    instead: Helen has more seniority than *anyone else* in the firm.

    not: Our house is older than *any* building on the block.

    instead: Our house is older than *any other* building on the block.

    The addition of *else* and *other* in the preceding sentences avoids the logical impossibility that Helen has more seniority than herself or that our house is older than itself. Likewise, it prevents the possible misreading that Helen is not a member of the firm or that our house is not on the block.

12. The antecedent of an indefinite pronoun—that is, the thing it is referring to—must be clearly stated, not implied. A good check for a clear reference is to see if there is an ante-

cedent in the sentence that could be substituted for the pronoun; if there is none, the pronoun should be replaced by a noun or nominal.

unclear: He's the author of a best-selling book on sailing, even though he's never set foot on *one.*

clear: He's the author of a best-selling book on sailing, even though he's never set foot on a sailboat.

Interrogative Pronouns

13. The interrogative pronouns *what, which, who, whom,* and *whose,* as well as combinations of these words with the suffix *-ever,* are used to introduce direct and indirect questions.

> *Who* is she?
> He asked me *who* she was.
> *Whom* did the article accuse?
> She asked *whom* the article accused.
> *Whoever* can that be?
> We wondered *whoever* that could be.

Personal Pronouns

14. Personal pronouns refer to beings and objects and reflect their person, number, and gender. Most personal pronouns take different forms for the three cases.

	nominative	*possessive*	*objective*
first person			
singular:	I	my, mine	me
plural:	we	our, ours	us

second person
singular: you   your, yours   you
plural: you   your, yours   you
third person
singular: he   his, his   him
            she   her, hers   her
            it   its, its   it
plural: they   their, theirs them

15. Though a personal pronoun agrees in person, number, and gender with the word it refers to, its case is determined by its function within a sentence. The nominative case is used for a pronoun that acts as a subject of a sentence or as a predicate nominative (but see paragraph 16 below). The possessive case is used for pronouns that express possession or a similar relationship. The objective case is used for pronouns that are direct objects, indirect objects, retained objects, objects of prepositions, or objective complements.

> *You* and *I* thought the meeting was useful.
> My assistant and *I* attended the seminar.
> Our new candidate will be *you.*
> We all had *our* own offices.
> He told my assistant and *me* about the seminar.
> She gave *me* the papers.
> Just between *you* and *me,* the meeting was much too long.
> I was given *them* yesterday.
> That makes our new candidate *her.*

16. The nominative case after the verb *to be* (as in "It is I" and "This is she") is preferred by strict grammarians, but the objective case (as in "It's me") may also be used, especially in spoken English.

> The only candidate left for that job may soon be *she* [or *her*].

17. When a personal pronoun follows *than* or *as*, and is the subject of an implied verb, it should be in the nominative case.

> He received a bigger bonus than *she* [did].
> She has as much seniority as *I* [do].

18. The suffixes *-self* and *-selves* combine only with the possessive case of the first- and second-person pronouns (*myself, ourselves, yourself, yourselves*) and with the objective case of the third-person pronouns (*himself, herself, itself, themselves*). Other combinations (such as "hisself" and "theirselves") are nonstandard and should not be used.

19. Personal pronouns in the possessive case (such as *your, their, theirs, its*) do not contain apostrophes and should not be confused with similar-sounding contractions (such as *you're, they're, there's, it's*), which do contain apostrophes.

> Put the contract in *its* file.
> *It's* an extensive contract.
> *Whose* turn is it?
> *Who's* going to go?

20. When *I* or *me* is used with other pronouns or other people's names, it should be last in the series.

> Mrs. Smith and *I* were trained together.
> He and *I* were attending the meeting.
> The memorandum was directed to Ms. Montgomery and *me*.

21. Some companies prefer that writers use *we* and not *I* when speaking for their companies in business correspondence. *I* is more often used when a writer is referring only to himself or herself. The following example illustrates the use of both within one sentence:

> *We* [i.e., the company] have reviewed the manuscript that you sent to *me* [i.e., the writer] on June 1, but *we* [i.e., the company] feel that it is too specialized a work to be marketable by *our* company.

22. While the personal pronouns *it, you,* and *they* are often used as indefinite pronouns in spoken English, they can be vague or even redundant.

vague:	*They* said at the seminar that the economy would experience a third-quarter upturn. [Who exactly is *they*?]
explicit:	The economists on the panel at the seminar predicted a third-quarter economic upturn.
redundant:	In the graph *it* says that production fell off by 50 percent.
lean:	The graph indicates a 50 percent production drop.

23. Forms of the personal pronoun *he* and, less frequently, the indefinite pronoun *one* have long been the standard substitutes for antecedents whose genders are mixed or irrelevant.

> Present the letter to the executive for *his* approval.
> Each employee should check *his* W-2 form.
> If *one* really wants to succeed, *one* can.

Many writers today who are concerned about sexism in language recast such sentences to avoid the generic use of the masculine pronoun.

> Present the letter to the executive for approval.
> All employees should check *their* W-2 forms.
> Each employee should check *his or her* W-2 form.

The phrases *he or she*, *him or her*, and *his or her* should be used sparingly, however, as they can easily become tiresome. (For more on avoiding the generic use of the masculine pronoun, see paragraph 9 on page 240.)

Reciprocal Pronouns

24. The reciprocal pronouns *each other* and *one another* are used in the object position to indicate a mutual action or cross-relationship.

> They do not quarrel with *one another*.
> Karen and Rachel spelled *each other* at the convention booth.

25. Reciprocal pronouns may also be used in the possessive case.

> The two secretaries borrowed *one another's* stationery.
>
> The president and his vice president depend on *each other's* ideas.

Reflexive Pronouns

26. Reflexive pronouns (formed by compounding the personal pronouns *him, her, it, my, our, them,* and *your* with *-self* or *-selves*) express reflexive action or add extra emphasis to the subject of a sentence, clause, or phrase. Reflexive pronouns are used when an object or subjective complement refers to the same thing as the foregoing noun or noun phrase.

> She dressed *herself.*
>
> The baby isn't *himself* this morning.
>
> They asked *themselves* if they were being honest.
>
> I *myself* am not concerned.
>
> The cook told us to help *ourselves* to seconds.

Relative Pronouns

27. The relative pronouns are *that, what, which, who, whom,* and *whose,* as well as combinations of these with *-ever.* They introduce subordinate clauses acting as nouns or modifiers. While a relative pronoun itself does not exhibit number, gender, or person, it does determine the number, gender, and person of elements that follow it in the relative clause because of its implicit agreement with its antecedent. Consider, for instance, the following sentence:

> People *who are* ready to start *their* jobs should arrive at 8:00 a.m.

In this sentence, the relative pronoun "who" refers to the plural subject "people" and acts as the subject of the relative clause "who are ready to start their jobs." Because it refers to a plural word, it acts like a plural word within its clause and therefore calls for the plural verb "are" and the plural pronoun "their."

28. The relative pronoun *who* typically refers to persons and some animals; *which* refers to things and animals; and *that* refers to persons, animals, and things.

> a man *who* sought success
> a man *whom* we can trust
> Seattle Slew, *who* won horse racing's Triple Crown
> a book *which* sold well
> a dog *which* barked loudly
> a man *that* we can trust
> a dog *that* barked loudly
> a book *that* sold well

29. *Which,* preceded by a comma, is used to introduce nonrestrictive clauses—that is, clauses that are not essential to the meaning of the nouns they modify. Either *that* or *which* can introduce restrictive clauses—that is, clauses that are needed to define the nouns they follow. However, many writers prefer to use *which* only with nonrestrictive clauses. (For more on restrictive and nonrestrictive clauses, see the section beginning on page 272.)

> The paneled doors, *which* cost less, were more popular.
> The doors *that* they had ordered were out of stock.

30. Relative pronouns can sometimes be omitted for the sake of brevity.

> The man [*whom*] I was talking to is the senator.

31. The relative pronoun *what* may usually be substituted for the longer and more awkward phrases "that which," "that of which," or "the thing which."

stiff: He was blamed for *that which* he could not have known.

easier: He was blamed for *what* he could not have known.

32. The problem of when to use *who* or *whom* has been blown out of proportion. The situation is very simple: standard written English makes a distinction between the nominative and objective cases of these pronouns when they are used as relatives or interrogatives. (For more on cases, see paragraph 15 on page 243.)

nominative case: *Who* is she?

Who does she think she is, anyway?

She thinks she is the one *who* ought to be promoted.

Give me a list of the ones *who* you think should be promoted.

objective case: *Whom* are you referring to?

To *whom* are you referring?

He's a man *whom* everyone should know.

He's a man with *whom* everyone should be acquainted.

In spoken English *who* is favored as a general substitute for all uses of *whom* except in set phrases such as "*To whom* it may concern." In speech, then, *who* may be used not only as the subject of the clause it introduces but also as the object of a verb in a clause that it introduces or as an interrogative.

Let us select *who* we think will be the best candidate.

See the manager, Mrs. Keats, *who* you should be able to find in her office.

Who should we tell?

33. *Whom* is commonly used as the object of a preposition in a clause that it introduces.

Presiding is a judge *about whom* I know nothing.

He is a man *for whom* I would gladly work.

However, *who* is commonly used to introduce a question even when it is the object of a preposition.

Who [rarely *whom*] are you going to listen to?

Who [rarely *whom*] do you work for?

34. While in speech the nominative form *who* can often be used in the objective case, the reverse is not true: the objective form *whom* cannot be used in the nominative case in either spoken or written English. Avoid such usages as "*Whom* do you suppose is coming to the meeting?" which result from a mistaken notion that *whom* is somehow always more correct.

35. In formal writing, the relative pronouns *whoever* and *whomever* follow the same principles as *who* and *whom*.

nominative: Tell *whoever* is going to research the case that . . .

He wants to help *whoever* needs it most.

objective: She makes friends with *whomever* she meets.

In speech, however, as with *who* and *whom*, case distinctions become blurred, and *whoever* is generally used (see also paragraph 32 above).

Whoever did she choose?

Verb

A verb is usually the grammatical center of a predicate and expresses an act, occurrence, or mode of being. Verbs are inflected (that is, altered) for agreement with the subject and for mood, voice, or tense.

Verbs exhibit the following features: inflection (e.g., *help, helps, helping, helped*), person (first, second, third person), number (singular, plural), tense (present, past, future), aspect (time relations other than the simple present, past, and future), voice (active, passive), mood (indicative, subjunctive, imperative), and the addition of suffixes (such as *-ate, -en, -ify,* and *-ize*). Some of these features are described below.

Inflection

1. Regular verbs have four inflected forms, produced by adding the suffixes *-s* or *-es, -ed,* and *-ing*. The verb *help* as shown in the paragraph above is regular. Most irregular verbs have four or five forms (for example, *see, sees, seeing, saw, seen*); and one, the verb *be,* has eight (*be, is, am, are, being, was, were, been*). If you are uncertain about a particular inflected form, consult a dictionary that shows the inflections of irregular verbs and inflections resulting in changes in base-word spelling.

> blame; blamed; blaming
> spy; spied; spying
> picnic; picnicked; picnicking

A dictionary should also show acceptable alternative inflected forms for any verbs with such forms.

bias; biased *or* biassed; biasing *or* biassing
travel; traveled *or* travelled; traveling *or* travelling

All such forms may be found at their respective main entries in *Merriam-Webster's Collegiate Dictionary, Tenth Edition.* There are, however, a few rules that will aid you in determining the proper spelling patterns of certain verb forms, as shown in the paragraphs below.

2. Verbs ending in a silent *-e* generally retain the *-e* before consonant suffixes (such as *-s*) but drop the *-e* before vowel suffixes (such as *-ed* and *-ing*).

   arrange; arranges; arranged; arranging
   hope; hopes; hoped; hoping
   require; requires; required; requiring
   shape; shapes; shaped; shaping

A few verbs ending in a silent *-e* retain the *-e* before suffixes beginning with vowels in order to avoid confusion with other words.

   dye; dyes; dyed; dyeing [*vs.* dying]
   singe; singes; singed; singeing [*vs.* singing]

3. One-syllable verbs ending in a single consonant preceded by a single vowel double the final consonant before suffixes beginning with vowels (such as *-ed* and *-ing*).

   brag; bragged; bragging
   grip; gripped; gripping
   pin; pinned; pinning

4. Verbs of more than one syllable that end in a single consonant preceded by a single vowel and have an accented last syllable double the final consonant before suffixes beginning with vowels (such as *-ed* and *-ing*).

> commit; committed; committing
> control; controlled; controlling
> occur; occurred; occurring

The final consonant is not doubled when it is preceded by either two vowels or a consonant.

> retrain; retrained; retraining
> respect; respected; respecting

5. Verbs ending in *-y* preceded by a consonant normally change the *-y* to *-i* before all suffixes except *-ing*.

> carry; carried; carrying
> marry; married; marrying
> study; studied; studying

If the final *-y* is preceded by a vowel, it remains unchanged.

> delay; delayed; delaying
> enjoy; enjoyed; enjoying
> obey; obeyed; obeying

6. Verbs ending in *-c* add a *-k* before a suffix beginning with *-e* or *-i*.

> mimic; mimics; mimicked; mimicking
> panic; panics; panicked; panicking
> traffic; traffics; trafficked; trafficking

Tense and Aspect

7. Verbs generally exhibit their simple present and simple past tenses by single-word forms (for example, *do, did*).

8. The future tense is expressed by *shall* or *will* or by use of the simple present or present progressive forms in a context that makes the future meaning clear.

> I *shall do* it.
> He *will do* it.
> I *leave* shortly for New York.
> I *am leaving* shortly for New York.

9. *Aspect* involves the use of auxiliary verbs to indicate time relations other than the simple present, past, or future tenses. The *progressive tense* expresses action in progress or future action. The *present perfect tense* expresses action that began in the past and continues into the present, or that occurred at an indefinite time in the past. The *past perfect tense* expresses action that was completed before another past action or event. The *future perfect tense* expresses action that will be completed before some future action or event.

> *progressive:*   is seeing
> *present perfect:*   has seen
> *past perfect:*   had seen
> *future perfect:*   will have seen

The perfect and progressive aspects can also be combined to produce special verb forms, such as *had been seeing*.

Voice

10. Voice enables a verb to indicate whether the subject of a sentence is acting (*active* voice) or is being acted upon (*passive* voice).

active: He *respects* the other scientists.
She *loved* the children.

passive: He is *respected* by the other scientists.
She *was loved* by the children.

Sentences can be changed from active voice to passive voice by making the object of the verb its subject and by adding a form of the verb *be* to the original verb's past participle.

active: Napoleon *bit* the mail carrier.
Conrad *will cook* the dinner.

passive: The mail carrier *was bitten* by Napoleon.
The dinner *will be cooked* by Conrad.

Mood

11. Mood indicates manner of expression. The *indicative* mood states a fact or asks a question.

He *is* here.
Is he here?

The *imperative* mood expresses a command or request.

Come here.

Please *come* here.

The *subjunctive* mood expresses a condition contrary to fact. While it is not used often today, the subjunctive mood does appear in clauses following the verb *wish* and in clauses introduced by *if*.

I wish he *were* here.

If she *were* there, she could answer that.

Transitive and Intransitive Verbs

12. Verbs may be used transitively or intransitively. A *transitive* verb acts upon a direct object.

She *contributed* money.

He *ran* the store.

An *intransitive* verb does not act upon a direct object.

She *contributed* generously.

He *ran* down the street.

As in these examples, many verbs are transitive in one sense and intransitive in another.

Verbals

13. A group of words derived from verbs, called *verbals*, deserve added discussion. The members of this group—the gerund, the participle, and the infinitive—exhibit some but not all of the features of their parent verbs.

14. A gerund is an *-ing* verb form that functions mainly as a noun. It has both active and passive voices. In addition, a gerund has other characteristics of a verb: it conveys action, occurrence, or being; it can take an object; and it can be modified by an adverb. In the following sentences, "typing" and "driving" are gerunds, "data" and "his workers" are their objects, and "daily" and "hard" are adverbs modifying the gerund.

> *Typing* tabular *data daily* is a boring task.
> He liked *driving his workers hard*.

Since gerunds function as nouns, nouns and pronouns occurring immediately before gerunds are generally in the possessive case.

> She is trying to improve *her skiing*.
> We objected to *their telling* the story to the press.
> I listened to the *bird's chirping*.

15. Participles, on the other hand, function as adjectives. They may occur alone ("a *broken* lawn mower") or in phrases that modify other words ("*Having broken the lawn mower*, he gave up for the day"). Participles, like gerunds, have active and passive forms.

active form: *Having failed* to pass the examination, he was forced to repeat the course.

passive form: *Having been failed* by his instructor, he was forced to repeat the course.

Participles, unlike gerunds, are not preceded by possessive nouns or pronouns.

We saw *them telling* their story to the press. [i.e., we saw them as they told]

We saw the *senator coming*. [i.e., we saw him as he arrived]

16. **Infinitives may exhibit active** *(to do)* **and passive** *(to be done)* **voice and may indicate aspect** *(to be doing, to have done, to have been doing, to have been done)*. **Infinitives may take complements and may be modified by adverbs. In addition, they can function as nouns, adjectives, and adverbs.**

noun use: *To be known* is *to be castigated*. [subject and predicate nominative]

He tried everything except *to bypass his superior*. [object of preposition "except"]

adjectival use: They had found a way *to increase profits greatly*. [modifies the noun "way"]

adverbial use: He was too furious *to speak*. [modifies "furious"]

Although *to* forms part of a complete infinitive, it may be merely understood rather than stated.

He helped [*to*] *complete* the marketing report.

Sequence of Tenses

17. **If the main verb in a sentence is in the present tense, any other tense or compound verb form may follow it.**

I *realize* that you *are leaving*.
               you *left*.
               you *were leaving*.
               you *had left*.
               you *will be leaving*.
               you *will leave*.
               you *may be leaving*.
               you *must be leaving*.

18. If the main verb is in the past tense, subsequent verbs in the sentence may not use the present tense.

I *realized* that you *were leaving*.
               you *left*.
               you *had left*.
               you *had been leaving*.
               you *would be leaving*.
               you *could be leaving*.
               you *might be leaving*.
               you *would leave*.

19. If the main verb is in the future tense, subsequent verbs in the sentence may not use the simple past tense.

He *will see* you because he *is going* to class too.
                         he *will be going* to class too.
                         he *will go* to class too.
                         he *has been going* to class too.
                         he *will have been going* to class too.

20. Most writers try to maintain an order of tenses throughout their sentences that is consistent with natural or real time; that is, present tense for present-time matters, past tense for past matters, and future tense for future matters. However, there are two common exceptions. First, when the contents of printed material are being discussed, the present tense is often used.

> In *Etiquette*, Emily Post *discusses* forms of address.
> This analysis *gives* market projections for the next two years.
> In this latest position paper, the Secretary of State *writes* that . . .

Second, in order to convey a sense of immediacy to a particular sentence, the present tense may be used instead of the future.

> I *leave* for Tel Aviv tonight.

21. The sequence of tenses in sentences that express contrary-to-fact conditions is a common problem. The examples below show proper tense sequences.

> If he *were* on time, we *would leave* now.
> If he *had been* [not *would have been*] on time, we *would have left* an hour ago.

22. At one time, *shall* was considered the only correct form to use with the first person in simple future tenses (*I shall, we shall*), while *will* was limited to the second and third persons (*you will, it will, they will*). Today, however, either form is considered correct for the first person, *shall* being slightly more formal than *will*.

> We *shall* give your request special attention.
> We *will* send the agreement out tomorrow.

Subject-Verb Agreement

23. Verbs agree in number and in person with their grammatical subjects. At times, however, the grammatical subject may be singular in form but the thought it carries may have plural connotations. Here are some general guidelines for such situations. (For discussion of verb agreement with indefinite-pronoun subjects, see paragraphs 6–10 on pages 239–41. For discussion of verb number as affected by a compound subject whose elements are joined by *and/or*, see paragraph 6 on page 223.)

24. Plural and compound subjects take plural verbs, even if the subject is inverted.

> Both dogs and cats *were* tested for the virus.
> Grouped under the heading "fine arts" *are* music, theater, and painting.

25. Compound subjects or plural subjects working as a unit take singular verbs.

> Lord & Taylor *has* stores in the New York area.
> Macaroni and cheese *is* our best-selling product.
> Five hundred dollars *is* a stiff price for a ton.
>> *but*
> Twenty-five milligrams of pentazocine *were* administered.

26. Compound subjects expressing mathematical relationships may be either singular or plural.

> One plus one *makes* [or *make*] two.
> Six from eight *leaves* [or *leave*] two.

27. Singular subjects joined by *or* or *nor* take singular verbs; plural subjects so joined take plural verbs.

> A freshman or sophomore *is* eligible for the scholarship.
> Neither freshmen nor sophomores *are* eligible for the scholarship.

If one subject is singular and the other plural, the verb agrees with the number of the subject that is closer to it.

> Either the assistants or the supervisor *has* to do the job.
> Either the supervisor or the assistants *have* to do the job.

28. Singular subjects introduced by *many a, such a, every, each,* or *no* take singular verbs, even when several such subjects are joined by *and.*

> Many an executive *has* gone to the top in that division.
> No supervisor and no assembler *is* excused from the time check.
> Every chair, table, and desk *has* to be accounted for.

29. The agreement of the verb with its subject ordinarily should not be changed because of an intervening phrase.

One of my reasons for resigning *involves* purely personal considerations.

The president of the company, as well as members of his staff, *has* arrived.

He, not any of the proxy voters, *has* to be present.

30. The verb *to be* agrees with its subject but not necessarily with what follows.

His mania *was* minimizing payrolls and maximizing profits.

Women in the workforce *constitute* an important field of study.

The subject following *There is, There are,* etc., must agree in number with the verb.

There *are* many complications here.

There *is* no reason to worry about him.

31. Collective nouns—such as *orchestra, team, committee, family*—usually take singular verbs but can take plural verbs if the emphasis is on the individual members of the unit rather than on the unit itself.

The committee *has* agreed to extend the deadline.

but also

The committee *have been* at odds ever since the beginning.

32. The word *number* in the phrase *a number of* usually takes a plural verb, but in the phrase *the number of* it takes a singular verb.

A number of errors *were* [also *was*] made.

The number of errors *was* surprising.

33. A relative clause that follows the expression *one of the/those/these* + plural noun takes a plural verb in conventional English, but in informal English it may take a singular verb.

> He is one of those executives who *worry* [also *worries*] a lot.

> This is one of those new printers that *create* [also *creates*] perfect copies.

Linking and *Sense* Verbs

34. Linking verbs (such as the various forms of *to be*) and the so-called "sense" verbs (such as *feel, look, taste,* and *smell,* as well as particular meanings of *appear, become, continue, grow, prove, remain, seem, stand,* and *turn*) connect subjects with predicate nouns or adjectives.

> He *is* a vice president.

> He *became* vice president.

> The temperature *continues* cold.

> The future *looks* prosperous.

> I *feel* bad about the loss of jobs.

> He *remains* healthy.

Sense words often cause confusion, since writers sometimes mistakenly use adverbs instead of adjectives following these words.

> *not:*　　This scent *smells nicely.*

> *instead:*　This scent *smells nice.*

> *not:*　　The new formula *tastes well.*

> *instead:*　The new formula *tastes good.*

Split Infinitives

35. A split infinitive is an infinitive that has a modifier between the *to* and the verbal (as in "to really care"). Some grammarians disapprove of them, and many people avoid them whenever they can. However, the split infinitive has been around a long time and has been used by a wide variety of distinguished writers. It can be useful particularly if a writer wants to stress the verbal element of an infinitive. For example, in the phrase "to *thoroughly* complete the financial study," placing the adverb immediately before the verbal element strengthens its effect on the verbal. The position of an adverb may actually modify or change the meaning of an entire sentence.

original:	He arrived at the office to *unexpectedly* find a new name on the door.
repositioned with new meaning:	He arrived at the office *unexpectedly* to find a new name on the door.

Very long adverbial modifiers that interrupt an infinitive are clumsy and should be avoided or moved.

awkward:	He wanted to *completely and without mercy* defeat his competitor.
smoother:	He wanted to defeat his competitor *completely and without mercy.*

Dangling Participles

36. Dangling participles are participles that lack a normally expected grammatical relation to the rest of the sentence. The standard error

occurs when the participial phrase with which a sentence begins is immediately followed by a noun or pronoun representing a person or thing different from the one described in the phrase. They are best avoided, as they may confuse the reader or seem ludicrous.

not: *Walking through the door,* her coat was caught.

instead: *While walking through the door,* she caught her coat.

             Walking through the door, she caught her coat.

             She caught her coat *while walking through the door.*

not: *Caught in the act,* his excuses were unconvincing.

instead: *Caught in the act,* he could not make his excuses convincing.

not: *Having been told that he was incompetent and dishonest,* the executive fired the man.

instead: *Having told the man that he was incompetent and dishonest,* the executive fired him.

             Having been told by his superior that he was incompetent and dishonest, the man was fired.

Participles should not be confused with prepositions that end in *-ing* (such as *concerning, considering, providing, regarding, respecting, touching*).

Concerning your complaint, we can tell you . . .

Considering all the implications, you have made a dangerous decision.

Touching the matter at hand, we can say that . . .

Phrases

A phrase is a brief expression that consists of two or more grammatically related words but that does not constitute a clause. (See also the section on Clauses beginning on page 270.)

Basic Types

There are seven basic types of phrases.

1. An *absolute phrase* consists of a noun followed by a modifier (such as a participle). Absolute phrases act independently within a sentence without modifying a particular element of the sentence. Absolute phrases are also referred to as *nominative absolutes*.

    He stalked out, *his eyes staring straight ahead.*

2. A *gerund phrase* includes a gerund and functions as a noun.

    Sitting on a patient's bed is bad hospital etiquette.

3. An *infinitive phrase* includes an infinitive and may function as a noun, adjective, or adverb.

    noun: To do that would be stupid.
    adjective: This was an occasion *to remember.*
    adverb: They struggled *to get free* of the mounting debt.

4. A *noun phrase* consists of a noun and its modifiers.

    The second warehouse is huge.

5. A *participial phrase* includes a participle and functions as an adjective.

> *Listening all the time with great concentration,* she began to line up her options.

6. A *prepositional phrase* consists of a preposition and its object. It may function as a noun, adjective, or adverb.

noun: *Out of debt* is where we'd like to be!
adjective: Here is the desk *with the extra file drawer.*
adverb: He now walked *without a limp.*

7. A *verb phrase* consists of a verb and any other terms that either modify it or complete its meaning.

> She *will have arrived too late* for you to talk to her.

Usage Problems

8. Usage problems with phrases occur most often when a modifying phrase is not placed close enough to the word or words that it modifies. The phrase "on December 10" in the following sentence, for example, must be repositioned to clarify just what happened on that date.

not: We received your letter concerning the shipment of parts *on December 10.*

instead: *On December 10* we received your letter concerning the shipment of parts.

> We received your letter concerning the *December 10* shipment of parts.

9. Dangling participial phrases represent a very common usage problem. For a discussion of dangling participles, see paragraph 36 on pages 266–67.

Clauses

A clause is a group of words containing both a subject and a predicate. A clause functions as an element of a compound or complex sentence. There are two general types of clauses: the *main* or *independent clause* and the *subordinate* or *dependent clause*. A main clause (such as "it is hot") is an independent grammatical unit and can stand alone. A subordinate clause (such as "because it is hot") cannot stand alone, and must be either preceded or followed by a main clause.

Basic Types

Like phrases, clauses can perform as particular parts of speech within the sentence. There are three basic types of clauses that have part-of-speech functions.

1. The *adjective clause* modifies a noun or pronoun and normally follows the word it modifies.

> The circus clown, *who was also a trainer*, was multitalented.
> I can't see the reason *why you're upset*.
> He is a man *who will succeed*.
> She brought the specialty *that you ordered*.

2. The *adverb clause* modifies a verb, an adjective, or another adverb and normally follows the word it modifies.

> They made a valiant effort *because the children were in danger.*
> *When it rains,* it pours.
> I'm certain *that he is guilty.*
> We accomplished less *than we did before.*

3. The *noun clause* fills a noun slot in a sentence and thus can be a subject, an object, or a complement.

subject:	*Whoever is qualified* should apply.
object of a verb:	I do not know *what his problem is.*
object of a preposition:	Route that journal to *whichever desk you wish.*
complement:	The trouble is *that she has no alternative.*

Elliptical Clauses

4. Some clause elements may be omitted if the context makes clear the understood elements.

> I remember the first time [that] we met.
> This view is better than that [view is].
> When [she is] on the job, she is always competent and alert.

Placement of Clauses

5. A modifying clause should be placed as close as possible to the word or words it modifies so as to ensure maximum clarity and avoid the possibility of misinterpretation. If intervening words impair the clarity of a sentence, it should be rewritten or recast.

awkward: The yellow flowers were arranged in the blue vase, *picked that morning.*

recast: *Picked that morning,* the yellow flowers were arranged in the blue vase.

Restrictive and Nonrestrictive Clauses

Clauses that modify are also referred to as *restrictive* or *nonrestrictive.* Whether a clause is restrictive or nonrestrictive has a direct bearing on sentence punctuation. (For more information on restrictive and nonrestrictive clauses, see paragraph 10 on pages 18–19 and paragraph 29 on pages 248–49.)

6. Restrictive clauses are essential to the meaning of the word or words they modify, and cannot be omitted without the meaning of the sentences being radically changed. They are not set off by commas.

Textbooks *that are not current* should be returned.

In this example, the clause "that are not current" restricts the subject to a certain kind of "textbooks," and thus is essential to the meaning of the sentence. If the restrictive clause were omitted, "textbooks" would not be limited at all and the sentence would convey an entirely different idea.

Textbooks should be returned.

7. Nonrestrictive clauses are not inextricably bound to the word or words they modify but instead merely convey additional information about them. Nonrestrictive clauses may be omitted altogether without radically changing the meaning of the sentence. They are set off by commas.

> Our guide, *who wore a green beret,* was an experienced traveler.

In this example, the nonrestrictive clause "who wore a green beret" does not limit the subject to a particular class of guide; it merely serves as a bit of incidental detail. Removal of the clause does not affect the basic meaning of the sentence.

> Our guide was an experienced traveler.

Sentences

A sentence is a grammatically self-contained unit that (1) expresses a statement (declarative sentence), (2) asks a question (interrogative sentence), (3) makes a request or command (imperative sentence), or (4) expresses an exclamation (exclamatory sentence).

Basic Types

Sentences are classified into three main types on the basis of their clause structure.

1. The *simple sentence* has one subject and one predicate (either or both of which may be compound).

> Clothing is costly.
> Silk and linen are costly.
> Silk and linen are costly and are sometimes scarce.

2. The *compound sentence* is made up of two or more main clauses.

> I could arrange to arrive late, or I could simply send my colleague.
> This commute takes 40 minutes by car, but we can make it in 20 by train.
> A few of the teachers had Ph.D.'s, even more had B.A.'s, but the majority had both B.A.'s and M.B.A.'s.

3. The *complex sentence* combines a main clause with one or more subordinate clauses (italicized in the examples).

> The committee meeting began *when the business manager and the staff supervisor walked in.*
> *Although the city council made some reforms,* the changes came so late *that they could not prevent these abuses.*

Construction

Grammatically sound sentences can be constructed by following some general guidelines.

4. Use connectives to link phrases or clauses of *equal* rank. When a connective is used to link phrases or clauses that are not equal, the resulting sentence may sound careless or clumsy, and may even be confusing.

not: I was sitting in on a meeting, and he stood up and started a long, rambling discourse on a new pollution-control device.

instead: I sat in on a meeting during which he stood up and rambled on about a new pollution-control device.

I sat in on that meeting. He stood up and rambled on about a new pollution-control device.

not: This company employs a full-time research staff and was founded in 1945.

instead: This company, which employs a full-time research staff, was founded in 1945.

Established in 1945, this company employs a full-time research staff.

5. **Create parallel, balanced sentence elements.** When clauses having unparallel subjects are linked together, the resulting sentence can be unclear.

nonparallel: The report gives market statistics, but he does not list his sources for these figures.

parallel: The report gives market statistics, but it does not list the sources for these figures.

nonparallel: We are glad to have you as our client, and please call on us whenever you need help.

parallel:	We are glad to have you as our client, and we hope that you will call on us whenever you need help.
in two sentences:	We are glad to have you as our client. We hope that you will call on us whenever you need help.

6. Link sentence elements tightly together. When elements are strung together by loose or excessive use of *and*, the sentence can become too lengthy and may lack any logical flow.

not:	This company is a Class 1 motor freight common carrier of general commodities and it operates more than 10,000 tractors, trailers, and city delivery trucks through 200 terminals, and serves 40 states and the District of Columbia.
instead:	This company is a Class 1 motor freight common carrier of general commodities. It operates more than 10,000 tractors, trailers, and city delivery trucks through 200 terminals, and serves 40 states and the District of Columbia.

7. Choose the proper conjunction to link clauses. *And* is used to achieve simple linkage. However, if one clause is being contrasted with another, or if a reason or result is being expressed, a more specific conjunction should be used. (For more on coordinating and subordinating conjunctions, see paragraphs 1–6 and 10–12 on pages 220–26.)

too general:	The economy was soft *and* we lost a lot of business.

specific: We lost a lot of business *because* the economy was soft.

The economy was soft, *so* we lost a lot of business.

The soft economy has cost us a lot of business.

8. Avoid unnecessary or unexpected grammatical shifts, which can interrupt the reader's train of thought and needlessly complicate the material.

shift from active to passive voice: As we *finished* our tennis match, other players *were seen* coming onto the court.

rephrased: As we *finished* our tennis match, we *saw* other players coming onto the court.

shift in person: *One* can use either erasers or correction fluid to remove typographical errors; however, *you* should make certain that *your* corrections are clean.

rephrased: *You* can use either erasers or correction fluid to eradicate errors; however, *you* should make certain that *your* corrections are clean.

shift from phrase to clause: *Because of the current parts shortage and we are also experiencing a strike,* we cannot fill any orders now.

rephrased: *Because of a parts shortage and a strike,* we cannot fill any orders now.

9. Order the sentence elements rationally and logically. Place closely related elements as close together as possible.

related elements
separated: We would appreciate your sending us the instructions on shipping by mail or fax.

joined: We would appreciate your sending us by mail or by fax the shipping instructions.

We would appreciate your mailing or faxing us the shipping instructions.

10. Be sure that your sentences form complete, independent units containing both a subject and a predicate.

incomplete: During the last three years, our calculator sales soared. While our conventional office-machine sales fell off.

complete: During the last three years, our calculator sales soared, but our conventional office-machine sales fell off.

While our conventional office-machine sales fell off during the last three years, our calculator sales soared.

In dialogue or specialized copy, fragmentation may be used for particular reasons (for example, to attract the reader's attention).

See it now. The car for the Nineties ... A car you'll want to own.

Sentence Length

11. Sentence length is directly related to the writer's purpose; there is no magic number of words that guarantees a good sentence. An executive covering broad but complex topics in a long memo may use concise, succinct sentences for the sake of clarity, impact, and readability. An essayist who wants the reader to reflect on what is being said may employ longer, more involved sentences. A speechwriter may use a series of long sentences that build up to a climactic and forceful short sentence, in order to emphasize an important point.

Sentence Strategy

12. Coordination and subordination   Coordination involves linking independent sentences and sentence elements by means of coordinating conjunctions, while subordination involves transforming elements into dependent structures by means of subordinating conjunctions. Coordination tends to promote loose sentence structure; subordination tends to tighten the structure and to emphasize a main clause.

coordination: During the balance of 1995, this Company expects to issue $100 million of long-term debt and equity securities *and* may guarantee up to $200 million of new corporate bonds.

subordination: While this Company expects to issue $100 million of long-term debt and equity securities during the balance of 1995, it may also guarantee up to $200 million of new corporate bonds.

13. Interrupting elements Interrupting the normal flow of a sentence by inserting comments can be a useful way to call attention to an aside, to emphasize a word or phrase, to convey a particular tone (such as forcefulness), or to make the prose a little more informal.

> His evidence, if reliable, could send our client to prison.
> These companies—ours as well as theirs—must show more profits.
> This, ladies and gentlemen, is the prime reason for your cost overruns. I trust it will not happen again?

Interrupting elements should not be overused, however, since too many of them may distract the reader.

14. Parallelism and balance Parallelism and balance work together to maintain an even, rhythmic flow of thought. Parallelism means a similarity in construction of adjacent phrases and clauses that are equivalent, similar, or opposed in meaning.

These ecological problems are of crucial concern *to* scientists, *to* businesspeople, *to* government officials, and *to* all citizens.

Our attorneys have argued *that* the trademark is ours, *that* our rights have been violated, and *that* appropriate compensation is required.

He was respected not only *for his intelligence* but also *for his integrity.*

The thing that interested me ... about New York ... was the ... contrast it showed between the dull and the shrewd, the strong and the weak, the rich and the poor, the wise and the ignorant. . . .

— Theodore Dreiser

Balance involves the symmetrical use of two or more parallel phrases or clauses that contain similar, contrasting, or opposing ideas.

To err is human; to forgive, divine.
—-Alexander Pope

Ask not what your country can do for you—ask what you can do for your country.
—John F. Kennedy

15. Periodic and cumulative sentences Longer sentences can often be classified as either periodic or cumulative. The periodic sentence is structured so that its main idea or thrust is suspended until the very end, thereby drawing the reader's eye and mind along to an emphatic conclusion. In the example below, the main point follows the final comma.

Although the Commission would like to give its licensees every encouragement to experiment on their own initiative with new and innovative means of providing access to their stations for the discussion of important public issues, it cannot justify imposing a specific right of access by government fiat.

The cumulative sentence, on the other hand, is structured so that its main point appears first, followed by other phrases or clauses expanding on or supporting it. In the following example, the main point precedes the first comma.

The balance must be finely crafted, lest strategists err too much on the side of technological sophistication only to find that U.S. military forces can be defeated by overwhelming mass.

The final phrase or clause in a cumulative sentence theoretically could be deleted without changing the essential meaning of the sentence. A cumulative sentence is therefore more loosely structured than a periodic sentence.

16. **Reversal**   A reversal of customary or expected sentence order can be an effective stylistic strategy when used sparingly.

customary or expected order: These realities are indisputable: the economy has taken a dramatic downturn, costs on all fronts have soared, and jobs are at a premium.

reversal: That the economy has taken a dramatic downturn; that costs on all fronts have soared; that jobs are at a premium—these are indisputable realities.

17. **Rhetorical questions** The rhetorical question is yet another device to focus the reader's attention on a problem or an issue. The rhetorical question requires no specific response from the reader but often merely sets up the introduction of the writer's own view. A rhetorical question may serve as a topic sentence in a paragraph, or a series of rhetorical questions may spotlight pertinent issues.

> What can be done to correct the problem? Two things, to begin with: never discuss cases out of the office, and never allow a visitor to see the papers on your desk.

18. **Variety** Any kind of repetitious pattern may create monotony. As a means of keeping the reader's attention, try to maintain a balance of different kinds of sentences. Use a combination of simple, compound, and complex sentences in a paragraph, including a variety of short and long sentences. Vary the beginnings of your sentences so that every one does not begin directly with the subject. Through judicious use of combinations of sentence patterns and the sentence strategies discussed in the preceding paragraphs, you can attain an interesting, diversified style.

Paragraphs

The underlying structure of any written communication must be controlled by the writer if the material is to be clear, coherent, and effective. Since good paragraphing is a means to this end, the writer should be able to recognize various kinds of paragraphs and their functions, as well as problems that might arise from faulty paragraphing and discrepancies that could cause misinterpretation or detract from the effect of the communication.

1. A paragraph is a subdivision in writing that consists of one or more sentences, deals with one or more ideas, or quotes a speaker or a source. The first line of a paragraph is indented in reports, studies, articles, theses, and books; in business letters and memos it may or may not be indented, depending on the style being followed.

2. Paragraphs should not be considered as isolated, self-contained units that can be mechanically lined up without transitions or interrelationship of ideas. Rather, they should be viewed as components of larger sections that are tightly interlinked and that interact in the sequential development of a major idea or cluster of ideas. The overall coherence of a communication depends on this interaction.

Developing Paragraphs

3. Depending on the writer's intentions, paragraph development may take any of several directions. A paragraph may:

- Move from the general to the specific.
- Move from the specific to the general.
- Exhibit an alternating order of comparison and contrast.
- Chronicle events in order.
- Describe something (such as a group of objects) in a particular spatial order—for example, from near to far, or vice versa.
- Follow a climactic sequence, with the least important facts or examples described first, leading to the most important facts or examples. Or the facts or issues that are easy to comprehend or accept may be set forth first, followed by those that are more difficult to comprehend or accept. In this way the easier material makes the reader receptive and prepares him or her for the more difficult points.
- Follow an anticlimactic order, setting forth the most persuasive arguments first so that the reader, having been influenced in a positive way, is carried along by the rest of the argument with a growing feeling of assent.

Effective Paragraphing

4. A topic sentence—a key sentence to which the other sentences in the paragraph are related—may be placed either at the beginning or at the end of a paragraph. A lead-in topic

sentence should present the main idea of the paragraph and set the tone of the material that follows. A terminal topic sentence should be an analysis, conclusion, or summation of what has gone before it.

5. A single-sentence paragraph can be used to achieve an easy transition from a preceding to a subsequent paragraph (especially when the paragraphs are long and complex) if it repeats an important word or phrase from the preceding paragraph, contains a pronoun reference to a key individual mentioned in a preceding paragraph, or is introduced by an appropriate conjunction that tightly connects the paragraphs.

6. **Opening paragraph** The very first paragraph should set the tone, introduce the subject, and lead into the discussion. It should be worded so as to immediately attract attention and arouse interest. Opening paragraphs of the following kinds can be effective:

- a succinct statement of purpose or point of view
- a concise definition of a problem
- a lucid statement of a key issue or fact

Openings of the following kinds, by contrast, can blunt the point of the rest of the material:

- an apology for the material to be presented
- a querulous complaint or a defensive posture
- a detailed account of material presented earlier
- a presentation of self-evident facts

- a group of sentences rendered limp and meaningless by clichés

7. **Closing paragraph** The last paragraph ties together all the ideas and points that have been set forth earlier and reemphasizes the main thrust of the communication. Effective endings can be of several types:

- a setting forth of the most important conclusions drawn from the preceding discussion
- a final analysis of the main problems under discussion
- a lucid summary of the individual points brought up earlier
- a final, clear statement of opinion or position
- concrete suggestions or solutions, if applicable
- specific questions asked of the reader, if applicable

Endings of the following kinds, by contrast, can reduce the effect of a communication:

- apologies for a poor presentation
- qualifying remarks that blunt or negate incisive points made earlier
- insertion of minor details or afterthoughts
- a meaningless closing couched in clichés

Criteria

8. The following are tests of good paragraphs:

- Does the paragraph have a clear purpose, or is it there just to fill up space? Does it simply restate in other terms what has been said before?

- Does the paragraph clarify rather than cloud the main ideas of the piece?
- Is the paragraph adequately developed, or does it merely raise other questions that it does not attempt to answer? If a position is being taken, are supporting information and statistics essential to its defense included?
- Are the length and wording of the paragraphs sufficiently varied, or is the same language used again and again?
- Is the sentence structure within each paragraph coherent?
- Is each paragraph unified and coherent? Do all the sentences really *belong* there, or do they digress into areas that would have been better covered in another paragraph or omitted altogether? Does each sentence lead clearly and logically to the next?
- Are the transitions between paragraphs achieved by transitional phrases that indicate the relationship between them and indicate the direction in which the presentation is moving?

Chapter 7

Notes and Bibliographies

Writers and editors use various methods to indicate the source of a quotation or piece of information borrowed from another work.

In works published for the general public, and traditionally in scholarly works in the humanities, footnotes or endnotes have been preferred. In this system, sequential numbers within the text refer the reader to notes at the bottom of the page or at the end of the article, chapter, or book; these notes contain full bibliographic information on the works cited.

In scholarly works in the social and natural sciences, and increasingly in the humanities as well, parenthetical references within the text refer the reader to an alphabetically arranged list of references at the end of the work.

The system of footnotes or endnotes is the more flexible, in that it allows for commentary on the work or subject and can also be used for brief peripheral discussions not tied to any specific work. However, style manuals tend to encourage the use of parenthetical references in addition to or instead of footnotes or endnotes, since for most kinds of material they are efficient and convenient for both writer and reader.

In a carefully documented work, a bibliography or list of references normally follows the entire text (including any endnotes), regardless of which system is used.

Though different publishers and journals have adopted slightly varying styles, the following examples illustrate standard styles for footnotes, endnotes, parenthetical references, and bibliographic entries. For more extensive treatment than can be provided here, consult *Merriam-Webster's Standard American Style Manual*, *The Chicago Manual of Style*, *The MLA Handbook for Writers of Research Papers*, or *Scientific Style and Format: The CBE Manual for Authors, Editors, and Publishers*.

Footnotes and Endnotes

Footnotes and endnotes are usually indicated by unpunctuated Arabic superior numbers placed immediately after the material to be documented. The number is placed at the end of a sentence or clause, or at some other natural break in the sentence; it follows all marks of punctuation except the dash.

> As some researchers noted, "New morphological, biochemical, and karyological studies suggest that *P. boylii* actually comprises several distinct species,"[12] and. . . .

The numbering is consecutive throughout an article or monograph; in a book, it usually starts over with each new chapter or section.

The text of the note itself is introduced with the corresponding number. Footnotes appear at the bottom of the page; endnotes, which take the same form as footnotes, are gathered at the end of the article, chapter, or book.

Endnotes are generally preferred over footnotes by writers and publishers because they are easier to handle when preparing both manuscript and printed pages, though they can be less convenient for the reader.

Both footnotes and endnotes provide full bibliographic information for a source the first time it is cited. In subsequent references, this information is shortened to the author's last name and the page number (if more than one book by an author is cited, a shortened form of the title is also included); less frequently, the Latin abbreviation *ibid.* is used to refer to the book cited in the immediately preceding note.

The following examples describe specific elements of first references and reflect humanities citation style; notes 14–16 show examples of subsequent references. All of the cited works appear again in the Bibliographies and Lists of References section beginning on page 296.

Books

One author:

1. Elizabeth Bishop, *The Complete Poems: 1927–1979* (New York: Farrar, Straus & Giroux, 1983), 46.

Two or three authors:

2. Bert Hölldobler and Edward O. Wilson, *The Ants* (Cambridge, Mass.: Belknap–Harvard Univ. Press, 1990), 119.

3. Charles T. Brusaw, Gerald J. Alred, and Walter E. Oliu, *The Business Writer's Handbook,* 4th rev. ed. (New York: St. Martin's, 1993), 182–84.

Four or more authors:

4. Randolph Quirk et al., *A Comprehensive Grammar of the English Language* (London: Longman, 1985), 135.

Corporate author:

5. Commission on the Humanities, *The Humanities in American Life* (Berkeley: Univ. of California Press, 1980), 58.

No author:

6. *Information Please Almanac: 1995* (Boston: Houghton Mifflin, 1994), 324.

Editor and/or translator:

7. Arthur S. Banks, ed., *Political Handbook of the World: 1994–1995* (Binghamton, N.Y.: CSA Publications, 1995), 293–95.

8. Simone de Beauvoir, *The Second Sex,* trans. and ed. H. M. Parshley (New York: Knopf, 1953; Vintage, 1989), 446.

Part of a book:	9. Ernst Mayr, ''Processes of Speciation in Animals,'' *Mechanisms of Speciation*, ed. C. Barigozzi (New York: Alan R. Liss, 1982), 1–3.
Name of a series:	10. George W. Stocking, Jr., ed., *Functionalism Historicized: Essays on British Social Anthropology*, vol. 2, History of Anthropology Series (Madison: Univ. of Wisconsin Press, 1988), 173–74.
Second or later edition:	11. Albert C. Baugh and Thomas Cable, *A History of the English Language*, 4th ed. (Englewood Cliffs, N.J.: Prentice Hall, 1992), 14.
Two or more volumes:	12. Ronald M. Nowak, *Walker's Mammals of the World*, 5th ed., 2 vols. (Baltimore: Johns Hopkins Univ. Press, 1991), 2: 661.
No publication data:	13. *Photographic View Album of Cambridge* [England], n.p., n.d., n.pag.
Subsequent references:	14. Nowak, 662.
	15. Baugh and Cable, *History*, 18–19.
	16. Ibid., 23.

Articles

A footnote or endnote referring to an article in a periodical is similar in form to one citing a book reference. The title of the article is enclosed in quotation marks, and the date and pagination of the article cited follow the form the periodical uses.

Weekly magazine:

17. Richard Preston, "A Reporter at Large: Crisis in the Hot Zone," *New Yorker*, Oct. 26, 1992: 58.

Monthly magazine:

18. John Lukacs, "The End of the Twentieth Century," *Harper's*, Jan. 1993: 40.

Journal paginated by issue:

19. Roseann Duenas Gonzalez, "Teaching Mexican American Students to Write: Capitalizing on the Culture," *English Journal* 71, no. 7 (Nov. 1982): 22–24.

Journal paginated by volume:

20. Stephen Jay Gould and Niles Eldredge, "Punctuated Equilibria: The Tempo and Mode of Evolution Reconsidered," *Paleobiology* 3 (1977): 121.

Newspaper:

21. William J. Broad, "Big Science Squeezes Small-Scale Researchers," *New York Times*, Dec. 29, 1992: C1.

Signed review:

22. Gordon Craig, review of *The Wages of Guilt: Memories of War in Germany and Japan*, by Ian Buruma, *New York Review of Books*, July 14, 1994: 43–45.

Subsequent reference:

23. Gonzalez, 23.

Parenthetical References

Parenthetical references are highly abbreviated bibliographic citations that appear within the text itself, enclosed in parentheses. Such references direct the reader to a detailed bibliography or list of references at the end of the work, often removing the need for footnotes or endnotes.

A parenthetical reference is placed immediately after the quotation or piece of information whose source it refers to, and punctuation not associated with a quotation is placed after the reference.

> As some researchers noted, "New morphological, biochemical, and karyological studies suggest that *P. boylii* actually comprises several distinct species" (Nowak 1991, 2:661), and. . . .

Any element of a reference that is clear from the context of the running text may be omitted.

> As Nowak observed, "Although these mice are among the most abundant of mammals, some forms have suffered through human activity" (662).

Parenthetical references in the humanities usually include only the author's (or editor's) last name and a page reference. In the social and natural sciences, the year of publication is included after the author's name with no intervening punctuation, and the page number is often omitted. This scientific style is commonly referred to as the "author-date system."

To distinguish among cited works published by the same author, the author's name may be followed by the specific work's title, which is usually shortened. (If the author-date system is being used, a lowercase letter can be added after the year—e.g., 1992a, 1992b—to distinguish between works published in the same year.)

Each of the following references is keyed to an entry in the bibliographic listings on pages 297–99.

Humanities style:	(Bishop 46)
	(Quirk et al. 135)
	(Baugh and Cable, *History* 14)
	(Comm. on the Humanities 58)
Sciences style:	(Mayr 1982, 1–3)
	(Stocking 1988, 173–74)
(without page nos.)	(Gould and Eldredge 1977)
	(Banks 1995a)

Bibliographies and Lists of References

A *bibliography* lists all of the works that a writer has found relevant in writing the text. A *list of references* includes only works specifically mentioned in the text or from which a particular quotation or piece of information was taken. In all other respects, the two listings are identical. They both appear at the end of the text, and are punctuated and capitalized in the same way.

Bibliographies and lists of references both differ from bibliographic endnotes in that their entries are unnumbered, are arranged in alphabetical order, and use different patterns of indention and punctuation. Entries for periodical articles also list their inclusive page numbers. The following bibliographic lists of cited works illustrate standard styles employed in, respectively, the humanities and the social and natural sciences.

The principal differences between the two styles are these: In the sciences, (1) an initial is generally used instead of the author's first name, (2) the date is placed directly after the author's name, (3) all words in titles are lowercased except the first word and the first word of any subtitle as well as proper nouns and adjectives, and (4) article titles are not set off by quotation marks. (In some scientific publications, the author's first and middle initials are closed up without any punctuation, and book and journal titles are frequently not italicized.) The following bibliographic lists include both books and periodical articles.

Humanities style

Baugh, Albert C., and Thomas Cable. *A History of the English Language*. 4th ed. Englewood Cliffs, N.J.: Prentice Hall, 1992.

Beauvoir, Simone de. *The Second Sex*. Trans. and ed. H. M. Parshley. New York: Alfred A. Knopf, 1953; Vintage, 1989.

Bishop, Elizabeth. *The Complete Poems: 1927–1979*. New York: Farrar, Straus & Giroux, 1983.

Brusaw, Charles T., Gerald J. Alred, and Walter E. Oliu. *The Business Writer's Handbook*. 4th rev. ed. New York: St. Martin's, 1993.

Commission on the Humanities. *The Humanities in American Life*. Berkeley: University of California Press, 1980.

Craig, Gordon. Review of *The Wages of Guilt: Memories of War in Germany and Japan*, by Ian Buruma. *New York Review of Books*, July 14, 1994: 43–45.

Gonzalez, Roseann Duenas. "Teaching Mexican American Students to Write: Capitalizing on the Culture." *English Journal* 71, no. 7 (November 1982): 22–24.

Lukacs, John. "The End of the Twentieth Century." *Harper's*, January 1993: 39–58.

Photographic View Album of Cambridge [England]. N.d., n.p., n. pag.

Quirk, Randolph, Sidney Greenbaum, Geoffrey Leech, and Jan Svartvik. *A Comprehensive Grammar of the English Language*. London: Longman, 1985.

Sciences style

Banks, A. S., ed. 1995. *Political handbook of the world: 1994–1995*. Binghamton, N.Y.: CSA Publications.

Broad, W. J. 1992. Big science squeezes small-scale researchers. *New York Times*, 29 Dec.:C1.

Gould, S. J., and N. Eldredge. 1977. Punctuated equilibria: The tempo and mode of evolution reconsidered. *Paleobiology* 3:115–51.

Information please almanac: 1995. 1994. Boston: Houghton Mifflin.

Hölldobler, B., and E. O. Wilson. 1990. *The ants*. Cambridge, Mass.: Belknap–Harvard Univ. Press.

Mayr, E. 1982. Processes of speciation in animals. *Mechanisms of speciation.* Ed. C. Barigozzi. New York: Alan R. Liss.

Nowak, R. M. 1991. *Walker's mammals of the world.* 5th ed. 2 vols. Baltimore: Johns Hopkins Univ. Press.

Preston, R. 1992. A reporter at large: Crisis in the hot zone. *New Yorker,* 26 Oct.:58–81.

Stocking, G. W., Jr., ed. 1988. *Functionalism historicized: Essays on British social anthropology.* Vol. 2. History of anthropology series. Madison: Univ. of Wisconsin Press.

Special Cases

Television and radio programs

Burns, Ken. *Baseball.* PBS. WGBY-TV, Springfield, Mass. 28 Sept. 1994.

Computer software

World Atlas. CD-ROM. Novato, Calif.: Software Toolworks, 1990.

Government publications

United States. Department of Labor. Employment and Training Administration. *Dictionary of Occupational Titles.* 4th ed. Washington: GPO, 1991.

U.S. Congress. Senate. Subcommittee on Administrative Law and Government Relations of the Committee on the Judiciary. *Hearings on Post-Employment Restrictions for Federal Officers and Employees.* 101st Cong., 1st sess. 27 Apr. 1989. H.R. 2267.

Congressional Record. 29 June 1993: S8269–70.

Index